Nelson Thornes

Othello

Nelson Thornes Shakespeare

Othello

Volume editor: **Steven Croft**

Series editors: **Duncan Beal and Dinah Jurksaitis**

Series consultant: **Peter Thomas**

Published in 2004 by:
Nelson Thornes Ltd
Delta Place
27 Bath Road
CHELTENHAM
GL53 7TH
United Kingdom

04 05 06 07 08 / 10 9 8 7 6 5 4 3 2 1

A catalogue record for this book is available from the British Library.

ISBN 0-7487-8601-5

Page make-up by Tech-set

Printed and bound in Spain by GraphyChems

Acknowledgements

Mary Evans Picture Library, pp. 3, 76; Royal Shakespeare Company ©, pp. 82, 176; Shakespeare Birthplace Trust, pp. 16, 30, 50, 66, 100, 112, 162, 190

Contents

Preface

The very name *Shakespeare* can overwhelm: so many associations with culture and history. We hope you will approach the plays with curiosity and a willingness to embrace the strangeness of Shakespeare's world: those quaint ways, weapons and words!

Our aim in the **Nelson Thornes Shakespeare** series is to provide a bridge between Shakespeare's world and our own. For all the differences between the two worlds it is intriguing to find so many similarities: parents and children; power games; loyalty and treachery; prejudice; love and hate; fantasy and reality; comedy and horror; the extremes of human behaviour. It is oddly moving to find that the concerns of the human race have not changed so much over the centuries, and that Shakespeare's themes are modern and recognisable.

The unfamiliarity of the language is best regarded not as a barrier, but as a source of interest. On the left-hand pages we have not only explained unfamiliar words, but have also drawn attention to aspects of wordplay, imagery and verse. The left-hand pages also have reminders that this is a piece of theatre, written to be performed and experienced visually. The **performance features** boxes invite you to consider such questions as: *How might this character react? What actions might be appropriate here? Try reading/acting this section in this way...* You are not fed one interpretation; you make the decisions.

To help you place individual scenes in the context of the whole play there is a **comparison feature** at the end of each scene: *Where else have we seen characters behaving like this? How do events in this scene parallel events two scenes back?* A brief **scene summary** brings together the main developments within that scene.

At the beginning of the play there are some **introductory essays** on background topics. They highlight aspects of Shakespeare's world which show a different outlook to our own: *How did they conduct courtship in his day? How has the status of the monarchy changed? What about their view of magic and the supernatural?*

A separate **Teacher Resource Book** contains material which will help deepen your understanding of the play. There are **worksheets** on individual scenes – valuable if you have missed any of the class study. They will also provide a good background which will help you demonstrate your knowledge in coursework essays. To this end, the book also contains some **Coursework Assignment essay titles** and hints on how to tackle them. The play and resource book together provide enough support to allow you to study independently, and to select the assignment you want to do, rather than all working together as a class.

Our aim is that you finish the play enthused and intrigued, and eager to explore more of Shakespeare's works. We hope you will begin to see that although ideally the plays are experienced in performance, there is also a place for reading together and discussing as a class, or for simply reading them privately to yourself.

Foreword

Who bothers to read introductions, especially introductions to plays by Shakespeare?

Well, you do, obviously, and that's a good start if you want to get more from your literature study. Reading this Foreword will help you to get more from Shakespeare's writing and from the accompanying material provided with the play.

Shakespeare – the great adapter

Shakespeare is regarded as a great writer but not because he was an original inventor of stories. His plays are nearly all adaptations of stories he found in books, or in history – or in somebody else's play. His originality came from the way he used this material. He changed his sources to suit himself and his audiences and was never afraid to change the facts if they didn't suit him.

The best way of understanding what Shakespeare thought valuable in a story is to look at the way he altered what he found.

The **Introductory essays** show how he changed characters or time-scales to enhance the dramatic effect or to suit a small cast of actors.

Shakespeare – the great realist

What Shakespeare added to his source material was his insight into people and society. He understood what makes people tick and what makes society hold together or fall apart. He showed how people behave – and why – by showing their motives and their reactions to experiences such as love, loss, dreams, fears, threats and doubts. These have not changed, even if we think science and technology make us different from people in Shakespeare's day. He was also realistic. He avoided stereotypes, preferring to show people as a complex mixture of changing emotions.

When you use the character sheets provided by your teacher, you will see this realism in action. His characters behave differently in different circumstances, and they change over time – just as we do in real life.

Shakespeare – the language magician

Shakespeare's cleverness with language is not just his ability to write beautiful poetry. He also wrote amusing dialogue, common slang, rude insults and the thoughts of people under pressure. He wrote script that uses the sounds of words to convey emotion, and the associations of words to create vivid images in our heads.

When you use the glossary notes you will see how his language expresses ugliness, hatred, suspicion, doubt and fear as well as happiness, beauty and joy.

Shakespeare – the theatrical innovator

Theatre before Shakespeare was different from today. Ordinary people enjoyed songs and simple shows, and educated people – the minority – enjoyed stories from Latin and Greek. Moral and religious drama taught right and wrong and there were spectacular masques full of music and dance for the audience to join in. Shakespeare put many of these elements together, so most people could expect something to appeal to them. He was a comprehensive writer for a comprehensive audience, writing to please the educated and the uneducated. He was the first to put realistic people from every walk of life on stage – not just kings and generals, but characters who talked and behaved like the ordinary folk in the audience. He was less interested in right and wrong than in the comedy or tragedy of what people actually do. *Only Fools and Horses*, and *EastEnders*, are dramas which follow a trend started by Shakespeare over four hundred years ago. He managed this in theatres which lacked lighting, sound amplification, scene changes, curtains or a large cast of actors.

The performance features accompanying the play text will help to show you how Shakespeare's stagecraft is used to best dramatic effect.

Whether you are studying for GCSE or AS, the examination is designed to test your ability to respond to the following:

1 Shakespeare's ideas and themes
2 Shakespeare's use of language
3 Shakespeare's skill in writing for stage performance
4 The social, cultural and historical aspects of his plays
5 Different interpretations of the plays.

1a. Showing personalities (ideas and themes)

Shakespeare thought drama should do more than preach simple moral lessons. He thought it should show life as it was, daft and serious, joyful and painful. He didn't believe in simple versions of good and evil, heroes and villains. He thought most heroes had unpleasant parts to their nature, just as most villains had good parts. This is why he showed people as a mixture. In *Hamlet*, he wrote that the dramatist should **hold a mirror up to nature**, so that all of us can see ourselves reflected. As he picks on the parts of human behaviour that don't change (fear, jealousy, doubt, self-pity), his characters remind us of people we know today – and of ourselves – not just people who lived a long time ago. This is because Shakespeare shows us more than his characters' status in life. He knew that beneath the robes or the crown there is a heart the same as any tradesman's or poor person's. He knew that nobody in real life is perfect – so he didn't put perfect characters on his stage.

Shakespeare's understanding of people is based on the view that the greatest in society can still be as vulnerable to human faults as the lowest. He shows Othello as a man admired for his bravery, skills in warfare and leadership but unable to cope with common emotions such as jealousy. He also shows how someone like Desdemona can be honest and faithful but distrusted because her husband trusts his friend more than he trusts her.

1b. Showing what society was/is like (ideas and themes)

In *Hamlet*, Shakespeare declared that drama should show the **form and pressure of the age**, meaning the structure of the times we live in and the pressures and influences it creates.

Elizabethan England had known great conflict and turmoil through civil unrest and was also always under threat from other countries (Shakespeare was 20 at the time of the Spanish Armada). It was also a nation changing from the old ways of country living. London and other cities were growing, and voyagers were exploring other lands. New trades were developing, and plague and disease spread quickly in crowded parts of the cities. Most people were superstitious, but science was beginning to make its mark. People still generally believed in the Divine Right of Kings, but they were beginning to think that bad kings may be removed for the country's good. One such example was Charles I who was executed only 33 years after Shakespeare's death.

People in different cultures hold their own values and preferences, and sometimes view other cultures as alien or inferior. Iago thinks of Cassio as a **mathematician** and a **Florentine**. This reveals the way people in Venice thought of themselves as practical and serious, and thought of people from Florence as intellectuals and overly fashion-conscious. On the other hand, attitudes can change under different circumstances. Venice, under threat from the Turks, is willing to exploit the Moor when it needs him, and put aside the anger and racist resentment of Brabantio, a senior politician. Brabantio has a grievance against the Moor who has, he thinks, stolen his daughter.

2. Shakespeare's use of the English language (sound and image)

Shakespeare wrote the speech of uneducated servants and traders but he could also write great speeches using rhetoric. Whether it is a dim-witted inn-servant called Francis in *Henry IV Part One*, or a subtle political operator like Mark Antony in *Julius Caesar*, Shakespeare finds words to make them sound and seem convincing.

Saying little can be as eloquent as saying a lot, as Iago demonstrates by sowing seeds of doubt in Othello's mind when he feigns reluctance to say more about Desdemona and Cassio: **Indeed? ... Honest, my lord? ... Think, my lord?**

3a. Writing for a mixed audience (writing for stage performance)

As a popular dramatist who made his money by appealing to the widest range of people, Shakespeare knew that some of his audience would be literate, and some not. So he made sure that there was something for everybody – something clever and something vulgar, something comic and something tragic.

Othello has moments of coarse sexual humour such as the scene at the beginning of the play when Iago and Roderigo taunt Brabantio about what is happening to his daughter. It also has scenes of tender and lyrical beauty such as the Willow scene. There is bawdy wit and humour in Iago's comments about women and in Desdemona's answers, and there is a nail-biting plot involving the handkerchief and what it comes to mean. It's a love story, a revenge story and a psychological thriller. Those who want a villain, a hero and a heroine will be pleased. So, too, will those who are unconcerned about a villain with whom they can feel some sympathy, a hero for whom they can feel some contempt, and a heroine who could do more to stand up for herself.

3b. Shakespeare's craft (writing for stage performance)

Shakespeare worked with very basic stage technology but, as a former actor, he knew how to give his actors the guidance they needed. His scripts use embedded prompts, either to actors, or to the audience, so that he did not have to write stage directions for his actors. If an actor says, **Put your cap to its proper purpose**, it is a cue to another actor to be using his hat for fancy gestures, rather than wearing it on his head. If an actor comes on stage and says, **So this is the forest of Arden**, we know where the scene is set, without expensive props and scenery.

4. Social, cultural and historical aspects

There are two ways of approaching this. One way is to look at what the plays reveal for us about life in Shakespeare's time – and how it is different from today. The other is to look at what the plays reveal for us about life in Shakespeare's time – and how it is the same today.

Looking at *Othello* from an Elizabethan perspective, it has much to say about the dangers of jealousy, false honour and misguided trust as tragic human flaws. Looking at it from a twenty-first century point of view, we can see the same things but we may see these things as products of a culture which is too masculine and too militaristic. The play presents events in Venice and Cyprus – distant places – but it also serves to remind us that some of the passions and frailties do not respect national or cultural barriers. They remain as strong and potentially good or destructive in England as in Venice, and in 2004 as well as in 1604.

Enjoy Shakespeare's play! It's your play, too!

Peter Thomas

Introductory essays

1 The source of the play, historical context and settings

The source

Shakespeare used many sources to provide ideas for his plays and a particular play might be based on, or be influenced by, several sources. In the case of *Othello*, though, it is likely that Shakespeare took ideas from a single source – *The Story of Disdemona of Venice and the Moorish Captain* by the Italian writer Giraldi Cinthio, published in 1566.

Although the general lines of the plot of *Othello*, as well as some of the characters and ideas, have some obvious connections with this story, Shakespeare makes a number of significant changes to his plot which transform a basically simple story into a far more rich and complex drama.

In Cinthio's narrative, the only character named is the heroine, Disdemona. The Moor of Venice, a brave military figure, falls in love with her and, even though there is opposition from her family, they are married. They live happily together in Venice until the Moor is ordered to take a contingent of soldiers to Cyprus. He takes Disdemona with him and they have a completely calm journey.

One of the Moor's soldiers is an ensign and he too is accompanied by his wife who is a good friend of Disdemona. There is also a captain with them and he is much liked by the Moor and spends a lot of time with him and Disdemona.

The Ensign, who everyone thinks is a courageous and reliable soldier, falls in love with Disdemona and tries all kinds of ways to seduce her but without success. He believes that she wants the Captain and so plots to get rid of him by telling the Moor that Disdemona has committed adultery with the Captain.

Various events follow involving the dismissal of the Captain for wounding a fellow soldier, the stealing of Disdemona's precious handkerchief and the manipulation of the Captain by the Ensign to convince the Moor of his wife's infidelity.

In the end, the Moor and the Ensign plot to beat Disdemona to death and cause the roof to fall in on her so that her death would look like an accident. The plan works and everyone is shocked and saddened by her death. After her death, the Moor becomes grief-stricken and feels hatred towards the Ensign and dismisses him. The Ensign vows revenge and forms an alliance with the Captain. They return to Venice and, based on information from the Ensign, the Moor is charged with the murder of Disdemona. The Moor is arrested and tortured but refuses to confess and is imprisoned and then exiled, eventually being killed by Disdemona's relatives. The Ensign is later arrested for plotting against one of his companions, is tortured and dies of his injuries.

These are some of the ways in which Shakespeare alters Cinthio's tale:

- In Cinthio's tale, the Moor is the commander of a contingent of soldiers whereas Othello is a general.

- The character of Roderigo does not exist in Cinthio's tale.
- In Cinthio's tale, the Ensign acts purely out of a jealous desire for revenge, whereas in *Othello* Iago's motives are much more complex.
- Details of Othello's courtship of Desdemona are added.
- Shakespeare expands the brawl scene making it much more significant.
- The storm scene is added.
- In Cinthio's tale, the action takes place over a much longer period than it seems to in *Othello*.
- In *Othello*, Emilia is unaware of Iago's plot, but in Cinthio the Ensign's wife knows all about it but is too afraid to say anything.
- In Cinthio's story, the Moor is much more easily tricked and the Ensign plots with him to kill Disdemona. They murder her but make it look like an accident by having the roof fall in on her. This crude melodrama is transformed into a much more subtle and complex tragic ending by Shakespeare.
- In Cinthio, the story drags on after the murder. The Moor does not kill himself and is eventually released and banished and is only killed long after by members of Disdemona's family seeking revenge.
- The Ensign also escapes justice and returns to his own country, but is eventually tortured for plotting against one of his companions and dies of his injuries.

To fully appreciate how Shakespeare has created a great tragedy out of this basic storyline, it is worth thinking about what has been gained by making the changes outlined here. Think about what each change adds to the dramatic effects achieved.

Historical context: the Cyprus wars

The play begins set against the background of Venice but the action quickly moves to Cyprus. In terms of the plot, the reason for the move to Cyprus is because of the attack made on the island by the Turks. To a modern audience, this may seem simply a device to move the action to a place where Othello can be in complete charge, where the action can take place away from the restraints of Venice. However, to the Elizabethan audience the conflict between the Ottoman Empire and the Christians was something which was of much more immediate interest. That conflict and the threats it posed to the Christian world was present throughout Shakespeare's life and continued into the late seventeenth century.

In the sixteenth century, Venice was a wealthy commercial centre and Cyprus was one of its rich possessions. However, it was far from Venice, and its location made it vulnerable to attack from the Turks who wanted to capture it and its riches for themselves. The Turks attacked and occupied part of Cyprus in 1570 and, after a long siege, gained total control of the island in 1571. A Christian fleet consisting of the combined forces of Venice, Rome and Spain destroyed the Turkish fleet at the Battle of Lepanto in 1571 but the island of Cyprus remained in Turkish hands.

The discussion of the intelligence reports on the Turkish fleet's movements received by the Senate in Act 1 seems to be based on accounts of the original events leading up to the first attack on Cyprus and many in Shakespeare's audience would be familiar with these events. However, as soon as the action moves to Cyprus, Shakespeare's focus switches completely away from historical events, and the wider political and military aspects of the play fade into the background as we hear that the Turkish fleet has been destroyed:

> **News, lads! Our wars are done.**
> **The desperate tempest hath so banged the Turks**
> **That their designment halts.** *(Act 2 Scene 1, lines 20–2)*

This is confirmed by Othello when he enters: **News, friends! Our wars are done: the Turks are drowned.** *(Act 2 Scene 1, line 192)*.

To the Elizabethan audience, the play's initial connections with actual events, at least in some respects, would have set it within a context that they understood. Having served their dramatic purpose, Shakepeare then disposes of these public events to focus on the more personal elements that are at the heart of the tragedy. He is interested in the plot and the development of the characters rather than historical events.

The Battle of Lepanto

The settings

Although the war against the Turks plays no further part in the play, it is worth thinking about the questions:

- Did Shakespeare simply use the Turkish attack as a reason for shifting all the action to Cyprus or does the opening of the play, set against the danger of invasion, contribute something more significant to the drama?
- Would the play lose anything from being set in a time of peace as Cinthio's story was (it was written before the Turkish attack)?

In many ways, the Turkish threat and the consequent shifting of the action to Cyprus contributes to the dramatic effect of the play in a number of ways:

Cyprus

- The threatened Turkish invasion creates a sense of tension and urgency.
- Although the threat is dispelled, Cyprus is an island on a war alert – notice how Othello is anxious there are no civil disturbances during the celebrations.
- When Othello enters and stops the brawl he emphasises this point clearly:

> **What! In a town of war,**
> **Yet wild, the people's hearts brim-full of fear,**
> **To manage private and domestic quarrel?**
> **In night, and on the court and guard of safety?**
> **'Tis monstrous!** *(Act 2 Scene 3, lines 192–6)*

- As Governor of Cyprus, Othello is in complete charge which makes him all-powerful and his descent into jealousy and brutality more effective and shocking.
- Cyprus is away from the order and civilised codes of Venice.
- The island lies between Christian civilisation and the pagan barbarism of the Ottomites, reflecting Othello's descent from civilised behaviour into barbarism. This transformation is suggested in his own response to the brawl when he asks:

> **Are we turned Turks, and to ourselves do that**
> **Which heaven hath forbid the Ottomites?**
> **For Christian shame, put by this barbarous brawl!** *(Act 2 Scene 3, lines 149–51)*

By contrast, the world of Venice in which the play opens presents a more ordered world in which civilised behaviour and adherence to the law appears to be the norm. This is clearly seen in Act 1 when Iago and Roderigo shout from the darkness to awaken Brabantio and tell him that he has been robbed of his daughter. His surprised response shows us that the idea of robbery and law-breaking is something not expected in Venice:

> **What tell'st thou me of robbing? This is Venice;**
> **My house is not a grange.** *(Act 1 Scene 1, lines 106–7)*

Even when the action moves to Cyprus, however, we never lose sight of the contrast between the civilised Venice and the hostile Cyprus where men can be attacked in the darkened streets and murder be committed without restraint. We are reminded of the connection between the two settings at various points in the play. Othello sends and receives letters to the Senate, and Lodovico arrives from Venice with the message that Othello is to be recalled. His response to Othello striking Desdemona again emphasises this contrast between Venice and Cyprus:

> **My lord, this would not be believed in Venice**
> **Though I should swear I saw 't.** *(Act 4 Scene 1, lines 224–5)*

This tension between the settings of Venice and Cyprus reflects the wider conflict between civilised behaviour and barbarity which takes place within Othello and which is at the heart of the play.

There was another, darker side to Venice and Venetian society, though. Apart from its reputation as a great commercial centre, bastion of civilised values and a city of culture, it was also associated with revenge murders, vendettas and vice. The kind of values that gave rise to Iago.

2 Race and colour in *Othello*

In choosing a black hero for his play, Shakespeare, in one sense, was simply following his source Cinthio in whose tale the central figure was a 'Moor'. It is certain, though, that black people were not unknown in the England of the late sixteenth century. Some had arrived in the country as a result of the various clashes with Spain and were either slaves or servants. It seems likely, then, that at least some of Shakespeare's audience would be aware of black people or 'blackamoors' as they were known. Also during this period, there was much interest in travel, exploration of the world and the tales that travellers brought back from various parts of the world. Very often such tales described tribal natives and detailed their savage behaviour, cannibalism and alien appearance. Othello himself had such tales to tell when he tells the Senate of Brabantio's eagerness to hear such stories:

> **It was my hint to speak – such was my process –**
> **And of the Cannibals that each other eat,**
> **The Anthropophagi, and men whose heads**
> **Grew beneath their shoulders.** *(Act 1 Scene 3, lines 141–4)*

There has been much debate about the term 'Moor' itself, which literally speaking is a generic term for a native of Morocco and was sometimes broadly used to describe a member of the Berber Muslim people of North Africa, as opposed to the term 'Negro', which was usually applied to black people from the central and southern parts of Africa. However, such distinctions were not made on the Elizabethan stage, and Africans in general were portrayed as black and the word 'Moor' was used as a generic term to refer to any African.

From the middle of the sixteenth century, explorers, adventurers and slave traders had begun to bring Africans back to England from their North Africa voyages and occasionally they were introduced into plays or masques to add a sense of the exotic or strangeness to the performance or presentation.

Throughout the play's history, until recent times, the character of Othello has been played by white actors 'blacking up' and modern performances of the play have adopted a wide range of interpretations of Othello's origin. Orson Welles played the role in the 1952 film version, and in 1964 Lawrence Olivier was heavily made-up to create a Negro appearance. A number of critics have commented on how the unforgiving camera close-up shots of this production highlight the problems of a white actor 'blacking-up'. In 1981 Anthony Hopkins, in the BBC Shakespeare version, was made-up to look more Arabian in appearance. The notable exception to this fashion for white actors playing the role came initially in 1930 when the black actor and singer Paul Robeson played Othello in a London production. He returned to the role for the 1943 Broadway production, in which he became the first black actor to play Othello with an all white cast on an American stage in what became the longest running Shakespeare production. In more recent years, it has become much less acceptable for Othello to be played by white actors. One of the most influential productions, which marked the move to Othello being played by a black actor, was the casting of Willard White in the 1989 Royal Shakespeare Company (RSC) production, followed by the American film actor Lawrence Fishburne in the 1995 film version and Ray Fearon in the RSC 1999 production.

Although other dramas of the period often featured black characters, these were generally presented in an unfavourable light and adhered to the stereotype of the time of being servile, or morally deficient, sexually degenerate and attracted to white women. Shakespeare himself had previously used black characters in two of his plays – Aaron in *Titus Andronicus* and the Prince of Morocco in *The Merchant of Venice*. Both of these characters, to some extent, confirm the racial stereotype of the time, although both of them also show the early signs that Shakespeare was also beginning to challenge such stereotypes. For example, in *Titus Andronicus,* Aaron is presented as an evil and sexually voracious character, who has an adulterous affair with Tamora, the defeated Queen of the Goths, later to become Empress of Rome. However, Shakespeare's presentation of him is more complex than this, as he is also shown in the role of a parent when Tamora has a son. The baby's colour immediately shows Aaron to be the father and Tamora sends the baby to Aaron to be killed but he refuses to harm the child. Instead, he develops a bond with his son and a more tender and loving aspect to his character balances the brutal and wicked elements.

In *The Merchant of Venice*, the Prince of Morocco, one of Portia's suitors, is presented in a much more favourable light than some of the other suitors but he begins by immediately drawing attention to his colour:

> **Mislike me not for my complexion,**
> **The shadowed livery of the burnished sun**
> **To whom I am a neighbour and near bred.** (The Merchant of Venice,
> Act 2 Scene 1, lines 1–3)

Portia, though, describes him as **this noble prince** and in presenting him as a character of important rank possessing a dignity not seen in the other suitors, Shakespeare again challenges the racial stereotype of the time.

Othello develops this conflict between presenting a stereotype and at the same time challenging it in a much more complex way. Here are some elements of the play which confirm the cultural prejudices of the time:

- Iago's description and references to Othello at various points in the play and his presentation to Brabantio of the 'black man, white woman' image
- Roderigo's willingness to accept Iago's evaluation of Othello
- the contrast between Brabantio's attitude to Othello when he thinks he is merely an 'entertainer' compared to his response to having him as a son-in-law
- Emilia's comments to Othello later in the play:

> Oh, the more angel she,
> **And you the blacker devil!** *(Act 5 Scene 2, lines 132–3)*
>
> **thou art a devil.** *(Act 5 Scene 2, line 135)*

- the various references linking blackness with the devil or evil or hell
- Othello's own comments about himself and his blackness:

> **Haply for I am black**
> **And have not those soft parts of conversation**
> **That chamberers have, or for I am declined**
> **Into the vale of years** *(Act 3 Scene 3, lines 260–3)*

- the savagery that he descends to.

On the other hand, Shakespeare also challenges these prejudices in the following ways:

- He presents Othello as a character with authority, dignity and nobility. This is emphasised through the poetry of some of Othello's language.
- Many of the other characters speak of their respect for Othello.
- He is civilised and courtly.
- Even though he claims that **Rude am I in my speech** *(Act 1 Scene 3, line 81)* (which would be in keeping with the stereotype) his speech shows that he is extremely eloquent and sophisticated in speech.
- The public attitude towards his marriage to Desdemona is generally favourable.

Critical opinion is divided about how Shakespeare uses this stereotype though, some adopting the view that, through the character of Othello, he confirms the cultural prejudices of the time, while others feel that he challenges them through his presentation of Othello. Whichever view is taken, one thing seems clear – one of the key aspects of the tragedy is that Iago's evil schemes transform Othello into the racial stereotype, jealous, violent and savage, although the play ends with a brief return to the old Othello giving the audience a final glimpse of the qualities he possessed.

3 The imagery of *Othello*

Imagery is important in creating a sense of the opposing forces and emotions at work in *Othello*. Shakespeare uses a number of recurring images throughout the play, creating a pattern which reflects and reinforces the action. Several of these images involve juxtaposing conflicting ideas. These are some of the key image patterns in the play:

- storm
- black and white
- angel/devil; heaven/hell
- animals
- darkness and light.

Storm imagery

What happens in the tragedy is symbolised in the imagery used to describe the storm which destroys the Turkish fleet at the beginning of Act 2. Othello and Desdemona must pass through this storm in order to reach the apparent safety of Cyprus. Cassio is the first to arrive safely and a gentleman reports that the lieutenant:

> ... **prays the Moor be safe; for they were parted**
> **With foul and violent tempest.** *(Act 2 Scene 1, lines 33–4)*

Although reunited after the storm, they will soon be parted again when hit by the 'emotional storm' created within Othello by Iago's scheming.

When Cassio arrives he urges the heavens to give protection to Othello:

> **Oh, let the heavens**
> **Give him defence against the elements,**
> **For I have lost him on a dangerous sea.** *(Act 2 Scene 1, lines 44–6)*

Later he tells Desdemona that:

> **The great contention of sea and skies**
> **Parted our fellowship.** *(Act 2 Scene 1, lines 92–3)*

The word 'fellowship' here suggests a strong bond of friendship between Cassio and Othello, but a bond that will soon be broken.

Treacherous and deceptive appearances and ensnaring the innocent are also suggested through the imagery here, as Cassio describes their perilous journey:

> **Tempests themselves, high seas, and howling winds,**
> **The guttered rocks and congregated sands,**
> **Traitors ensteeped to enclog the guiltless keel,** *(Act 2 Scene 1, lines 68–70)*

Later in the same scene, when Othello arrives he describes how his **labouring bark** climbed **hills of seas** *(line 177)* – an image that is echoed in Act 5 Scene 2 as Othello approaches his end:

> **Here is my journey's end, here is my butt**
> **And very sea-mark of my utmost sail.** *(Act 5 Scene 2, lines 267–8)*

He has passed through his personal 'storm' and has arrived at his journey's end.

Black and white

The marriage of black and white is central to the play and we are repeatedly reminded of this in the imagery. Much of this is presented through traditional stereotypes of white being associated with purity, innocence and the virginal, while black is associated with the devil, evil and corruption. This stereotype is reinforced at the beginning of the play by Iago when he rouses Brabantio:

> **Zounds, sir, you're robbed! For shame, put on your gown.**
> **Your heart is burst, you have lost half your soul.**
> **Even now, now, very now, an old black ram**
> **Is tupping your white ewe.** *(Act 1 Scene 1, lines 86–9)*

Even the Duke's comment, in defence of Othello, implicitly reinforces this image:

> If virtue no delighted beauty lack,
> Your son-in-law is far more fair than black. *(Act 1 Scene 3, line 284–5)*

Repeatedly Iago's comments associate corruption and evil with the image of blackness, when he speaks of his intentions towards Desdemona: **So will I turn her virtue into pitch** *(Act 2 Scene 3, line 321).*

Emilia uses it when she condemns Othello for the murder of Desdemona:

> Oh, the more angel she,
> And you the blacker devil. *(Act 5 Scene 2, lines 132–3)*

The effect of the repeated use of this imagery is to show the conflict between good and evil and the corruption of the one by the other. Iago, although 'white' in appearance, is inwardly 'black' and Othello, outwardly black, is, as the Duke has said, inwardly **fair** according to the Elizabethan idea of the stereotype. The central point of Iago's evil is that he transforms Othello's inner nobility to evil blackness. In doing this, he transforms his vision of the world so that instead of seeing goodness he sees only evil and corruption – white has become black when he believes that Desdemona has been unfaithful to him. He makes this point himself when he considers what Desdemona's supposed adultery has done to him:

> My name, that was as fresh
> As Dian's visage, is now begrimed and black
> As mine own face. *(Act 3 Scene 3, lines 382–4)*

However, in the final scene, we are reminded of Desdemona's innocence and purity, ironically through Othello's own words:

> Yet I'll not shed her blood,
> Nor scar that whiter skin of hers than snow,
> And smooth as monumental alabaster; *(Act 5 Scene 2, lines 3–5)*

Angel/devil; heaven/hell

Linked with the black/white imagery in the play is the contrast between forces of good and evil. This is emphasised by a range of images juxtaposing angel/devil and the closely linked heaven/hell. It is Iago who is really associated with the devil and hell although he suggests to Brabantio in the first scene that it is Othello who is the 'devil', when he tells him that **the devil will make a grandsire of you** *(Act 1 Scene 1, line 91)* and at the end of the play Emilia also refers to Othello as a devil. However, Iago recognises his own links with hell and the devil, as is clear from his soliloquy in Act 2 Scene 3:

> Divinity of hell!
> When devils will the blackest sins put on,
> They do suggest at first with heavenly shows,
> As I do now. *(Act 2 Scene 3, lines 311–14)*

Finally, this connection becomes clear to Othello, as the captured Iago is brought before him. Othello looks down at Iago's feet to see if he has the cloven hooves of the devil:

> I look down towards his feet – but that's a fable.
> If that thou be'st a devil, I cannot kill thee. *(Act 5 Scene 2, lines 285–6)*

When stabbed by Othello, Iago's response makes a further connection: **I bleed, sir, but not killed** *(Act 5 Scene 2, line 287)*. Othello then refers to him as a **demi-devil** *(line 300)*.

Desdemona, on the other hand, representing innocence and virtue, is associated with images of heaven and angels. When she arrives safely in Cyprus through the storm, Cassio suggests she has divine protection:

> **Hail to thee, lady, and the grace of heaven,**
> **Before, behind thee, and on every hand,**
> **Enwheel thee round!** *(Act 2, Scene 1, lines 85–7)*

Othello recognises the link between Desdemona and heaven when he feels: **If she be false, heaven mocked itself!** *(Act 3 Scene 3, line 275)*. And when he tells her that she will damn herself by swearing that she is his loyal wife, he tells her:

> **Come, swear it; damn thyself,**
> **Lest being like one of heaven, the devils themselves**
> **Should fear to seize thee.** *(Act 4 Scene 2, lines 34–6)*

Ironically, though, he also sees the innocent Desdemona as a devil. He calls her **Devil!** as he strikes her and repeats:

> **Oh devil, devil!**
> **If that the earth could teem with woman's tears**
> **Each drop she falls would prove a crocodile.**
> *(Act 4 Scene 1, lines 226–8)*

These patterns of contrast, black/white, heaven/hell, angel/devil, have the effect of lifting the 'domestic' tragedy, as this play is often described, to tragedy symbolising the conflict between universal forces of good and evil.

Animal imagery

From the start of the play, Iago describes Othello using animal imagery. He calls him a **Barbary horse** *(Act 1 Scene 1, line 111)*, an **old black ram** *(Act 1 Scene 1, line 88)* and tells Brabantio that Othello and his daughter are **making the beast with two backs** *(Act 1 Scene 1, line 116)*. This has the effect of de-humanising Othello, presenting him as a character lacking in sophistication and driven by lust.

As Iago's corruption begins to eat away at Othello's mind, Othello himself begins to use animal imagery to describe his feelings towards Desdemona. For example, he adopts the language of falconry to describe his suspicions about Desdemona's fidelity and what he will do if these suspicions prove to be true:

> **If I do prove her haggard,**
> **Though that her jesses were my dear heart-strings,**
> **I'd whistle her off, and let her down the wind**
> **To prey at fortune.** *(Act 3 Scene 3, lines 257–60)*

As jealous thoughts take further hold, his imagery becomes more graphic and unpleasant, as he focuses on himself and his own situation:

> **I had rather be a toad**
> **And live upon the vapour of a dungeon**
> **Than keep a corner in the thing I love**
> **For others' uses.** *(Act 3 Scene 3, lines 267–70)*

an image repeated later when he reflects how Desdemona, who was everything to him, has betrayed him:

> **But there where I have garnered up my heart,**
> **Where either I must live or bear no life,**
> **The fountain from the which my current runs**
> **Or else dries up – to be discarded thence,**
> **Or keep it as a cistern for foul toads**
> **To knot and gender in!** *(Act 4 Scene 2, lines 56–61)*

Iago primes Othello's thoughts with vivid images presenting Desdemona and Cassio as lecherous and lustful animals:

> **It is impossible you should see this,**
> **Were they as prime as goats, as hot as monkeys,**
> **As salt as wolves in pride,** *(Act 3 Scene 3, lines 398–400)*

an image with powerful and unsavoury sexual connotations, echoed in Othello's exclamation as he leaves after striking Desdemona: **Goats and monkeys!** *(Act 4 Scene 1, line 246)*.

Darkness and light

The play moves between darkness and light. Night and darkness in the play are associated with evil and deception and the hiding of truth. The importance of darkness is seen in Iago's soliloquy at the end of Act 1:

> **Hell and night**
> **Must bring the monstrous birth to the world's light.**
>
> *(Act 1 Scene 3, lines 376–7)*

The first Act takes place at night and darkness allows Iago to cover his deceptions and his obscuring of the truth. The storm's darkness immediately follows at the opening of Act 2, but as the storm dies away and stability appears to be restored, the action moves into the light of day. Night falls again as Iago engages once more in deception and manipulation, getting Cassio drunk and engineering his provocation by Roderigo. Again, symbolically, darkness obscures the truth. Ironically, the scenes, in which the total deception that undermines Othello are carried out, are in daylight (Acts 3 and 4). The remainder of the play moves back to night, as the final darkness descends. The darkness, which covers the attack on Cassio and the murder of Roderigo, is even more intense than the darkness of the opening scene. Othello enters the darkened bedroom carrying a torch. This image links Othello with Iago who was the only one to carry a torch in the darkness of the previous scene. The image also connects the death of Desdemona with the extinguishing of the light: **Put out the light, and then put out the light** *(Act 5 Scene 2, line 7)*.

Desdemona is the 'light' and the 'truth'. Once she has been killed her 'light' can never be rekindled. Othello's action in killing her will bring darkness upon him.

11

4 The structure of the play

It has been said that *Othello* has the simplest plot of all the tragedies – the playing out of Iago's plan and its consequences. Although the storyline may be simple, the play's structure is designed to create maximum dramatic impact. This is how the action develops:

Act 1

> *Scene 1*
> The introduction of Iago and his grievance
> The incitement of Brabantio

> *Scene 2*
> The introduction of Othello and his confrontation with Brabantio

> *Scene 3*
> The threat of the Turks
> Othello defends himself against Brabantio's charges
> Desdemona is introduced

Act 2

> *Scene 1*
> The storm and destruction of the Turks
> The arrival in Cyprus
> Iago's scheming begins

> *Scene 2*
> The destruction of the Turks is proclaimed and celebrations announced

> *Scene 3*
> Iago gets Cassio drunk
> Cassio attacks Montano
> Othello dismisses him as lieutenant
> Iago advises Cassio to get Desdemona to plead his case

Act 3

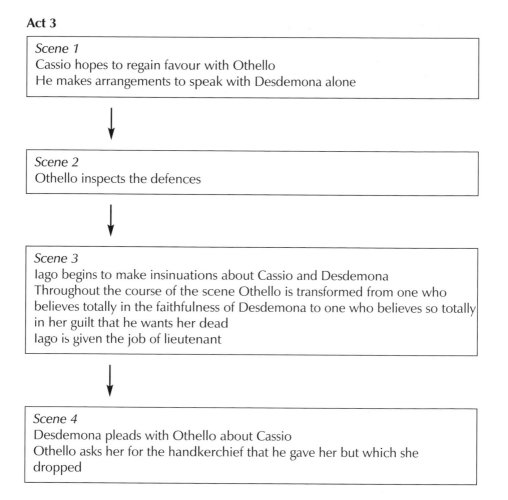

Scene 1
Cassio hopes to regain favour with Othello
He makes arrangements to speak with Desdemona alone

Scene 2
Othello inspects the defences

Scene 3
Iago begins to make insinuations about Cassio and Desdemona
Throughout the course of the scene Othello is transformed from one who believes totally in the faithfulness of Desdemona to one who believes so totally in her guilt that he wants her dead
Iago is given the job of lieutenant

Scene 4
Desdemona pleads with Othello about Cassio
Othello asks her for the handkerchief that he gave her but which she dropped

Act 4

Scene 1
Iago engineers it so that Othello can watch him talk to Cassio
Othello sees Cassio with Desdemona's handkerchief
He strikes Desdemona

Scene 2
Othello accuses Desdemona
Iago involves Roderigo in the plan to kill Cassio

13

> *Scene 3*
> Othello commands Desdemona to go to bed
> As she prepares for bed she discusses husbands with Emilia

Act 5

> *Scene 1*
> Roderigo wounds Cassio
> Iago kills Roderigo

↓

> *Scene 2*
> Othello kills Desdemona
> Emilia reveals the truth
> Iago is arrested
> Othello realises the truth and kills himself

The 'double-time scheme'

The plot develops rapidly and the action is fast moving, but it takes place within two quite separate timescales: 'short' time and 'long' time.
In the 'short' time scale:

- The first three scenes are continuous and take place in one night.

- There is an unspecified interval allowing for the journey from Venice to Cyprus.

- The three ships carrying Othello, Cassio and Iago, Desdemona and Emilia all arrive in the same day (Act 2 Scene 1).

- Othello's proclamation about the celebrations is read at 5.00 p.m. (Act 2 Scene 2)

- Cassio is involved in the brawl with Roderigo and Montano sometime between 10.00 p.m. and 11.00 p.m. (Act 2 Scene 3)

- The following morning Cassio speaks to Iago and both of them have been up all night. (Act 3 Scene 1)

- There could possibly be a time lapse between Acts 3 and 4 but dramatically the sense of continuity is strong.

- From the beginning of Act 4, the continuity to the end of the play is unbroken – the messengers from Venice arrive (Act 4 Scene 1) and are invited to supper **tonight**. The supper ends at the beginning of Act 4 Scene 3.

- Later in the evening – **between twelve and one** *(Act 4 Scene 2, line 222)* – Roderigo attacks Cassio and is killed by Iago.

- From here the action moves rapidly to Othello's murder of Desdemona.

This gives the impression of events unfolding rapidly, which is essential to create dramatic tension and give credibility to Iago's plot. It is vital to his plan that things happen quickly. If more time was available and Othello was able to speak to Cassio, the whole plan could fall apart. Iago is well aware of this when he says:

> the Moor
> **May unfold me to him – there stand I in much peril.** *(Act 5 Scene 1, lines 20–1)*

Obviously Iago is limited in the length of time he can keep the two apart, but a second time scale is running alongside, which suggests the passage of a much longer time than the first few hours presented through the action. This is the 'long' time scale:

- When Emilia finds the handkerchief she says:

  > **My wayward husband hath a hundred times**
  > **Wooed me to steal it,** *(Act 3 Scene 3, line 289–90)*

- Later in the same scene, Othello says:

  > **What sense had I of her stol'n hours of lust?**
  > **I saw't not, thought it not, it harmed not me;**
  > **I slept the next night well, was free and merry;**
  > **I found not Cassio's kisses on her lips.** *(Act 3 Scene 3, lines 334–7)*

- In Act 3 Scene 4, Bianca accuses Cassio who had apparently arrived from Venice only the previous day, of keeping away from her for **seven days and nights** *(line 163)*.

- When Othello falls into his fit, Iago tells Cassio: **This is his second fit; he had one yesterday** *(Act 4 Scene 1 line 50)* but he cannot possible mean the 'yesterday' when they arrived in Cyprus.

- In the final scene, Othello claims that Desdemona has:

  > **with Cassio hath the act of shame**
  > **A thousand times committed.** *(Act 5 Scene 2, lines 211–12)*

Why did Shakespeare use both a 'short' and 'long' time scheme? One possible purpose is to reconcile two apparently contradictory elements of the plot. In order for Iago to achieve his objectives before his plan is exposed, the action must take place over a short space of time, but a longer time is required for the alleged adultery between Desdemona and Cassio to have taken place. In performance, an audience is not aware of these contradictory elements, but is carried along with the fast-moving action of the plot and interaction of the characters.

5 Performance history and critical approaches

Othello: *a performance history*

The first recorded performance of *Othello* was in 1604 when it was performed in front of King James I at Whitehall. There are also records of it being performed again in April 1610 at the Globe Theatre at Bankside and further court performances in 1612 and 1613, 1629, 1635 and 1636. Theatres were closed during the Civil War but, when they re-opened in 1660, *Othello* was immediately performed again and, this time, the role of Desdemona was played for the first time by a woman. During Shakespeare's time, all female roles would have been played by boys.

During the eighteenth century, the play was heavily cut and altered to suit the tastes of the time. The role of Othello was often adapted, to make him seem either completely noble or wildly jealous. The popularity of the play continued through the nineteenth century, with a variety of famous actors playing the role of Othello. In 1814, Edmund Keen played the role in a performance described by William Hazlitt as 'the finest piece of acting in the world' and 'his heart seemed to bleed with anguish'. In this production, Keen emphasised the racial difference of Othello through ornate and exotic costume and jewellery. Keen also played the role of Iago and for some time alternated the parts. Desdemona also attracted famous actresses to the role, including Ellen Terry, who played the part in 1881 in a production in which the famous Victorian actor Henry Irving played Iago.

Two early twentieth-century performances emphasised Othello's 'difference' in another way. In 1901, Forbes Robertson wore armour, as well as a turban and ear-rings, to show both the military and ethnic aspects of the character. In 1919, F.J. Nettlefold went one step further and played the role dressed in a full suit of medieval armour.

Forbes Robertson as Othello in the 1901 production

In more recent years, several performances have been recorded on film, video and DVD. Orson Welles played Othello in 1952 and Laurence Olivier's National Theatre production in 1964 was also filmed. Although highly acclaimed in its time, Olivier's performance now seems dated. The lines are delivered in a highly dramatic and declamatory style which is not seen to the same extent in more modern and often more restrained performances. Also, in the medium of film, the viewer sees Othello in close-up, unlike on stage, and this reveals the problems of white actors 'blacking up'. Although the black actor and civil rights activist, Paul Robeson, played Othello in 1930 and 1944, it was not until the late 1980s that it became the norm to cast black actors in this role. In 1989, the black opera singer, Willard White, played Othello in the Royal Shakespeare Company's (RSC) production, in which Ian McKellen was Iago, Imogen Stubbs Desdemona and Zoe Wanamaker Emilia. A 1995 film version followed with Laurence Fishburne in the role of Othello and Kenneth Brannagh as Iago. More recently, Othello has been played by Ray Fearon in the RSC's 1999 production. In 2004 the RSC staged the play at the Swan Theatre, Stratford, with the South African actor, Sello Maake Ka Ncube, in the title role.

In recent years, actors have often been more interested in the role of Iago with the scope that it gives to exploring the complexities and ambiguities of the character. Ian McKellen, Kenneth Brannagh and Antony Sher have all presented their interpretations of this character in performances during the last few years.

Critical approaches

The range of interpretations, evident in the many productions of *Othello,* reflects the variety of critical interpretations applied to the play. Here are some of the critical approaches the play has inspired over the years:

- **Traditional criticism** In the early part of the twentieth century, the critic A.C. Bradley explored the analysis of characters in *Shakespearean Tragedy,* which had a big influence on the interpretation of the play. He (and other critics of this period) writes about characters as if they were real people, operating in settings which we, as a modern audience, could understand. The central point of his comments on Othello is that he is a noble Moor, a poetic character, largely blameless of the events which befall him. The whole tragedy comes about as a result of the scheming of Iago, who is seen as evil and wickedness personified.

  This view of the play has been extremely influential, but it has also been vigorously challenged. The critic F.R. Leavis, for example, saw Othello as a self-centred, self-dramatising figure, where there are important deficiencies, which are evident from the beginning of the play. Another critic, Helen Gardner, disagreed with Leavis, rejecting his psychological explanation for Othello's downfall. She sees Othello ruined by a loss of faith brought about by Iago's insinuations. It is interesting to note how these interpretations have been presented on the stage. Accounts of Paul Robeson's performance, for example, describe his presentation of Othello as emphasising the 'noble Moor' aspect of the character described by Bradley. Olivier's 1964 interpretation was more influenced by Leavis's view, rejecting the view of Othello as a noble man made jealous through his gullibility. Olivier's Othello brings out the character's vanity and tendency for self-delusion that was at the centre of Leavis's view.

  Differing views of Othello inevitably produce varying views of Iago also. Bradley sees him as dominant and corrupting. Leavis sees him as more a character simply serving a dramatic function.

- **Psycholoanalytical criticism** Later in the twentieth century, largely through the works of Sigmund Freud, psychoanalysis became a major influence on understanding and interpreting human behaviour and motivation. Freud explained personality in terms of a range of unconscious factors involving repressed desires, anxieties, sexual urges, conflicts, and so forth. Some critics adapted this approach to the analysis of characters in the play. This approach has given rise to a range of ideas, particularly concerning Iago's sexual attitudes. It has been suggested that he is a latent homosexual, jealous of those close to Othello, and desiring to control him. This approach was taken in the 1985 RSC production, in which Ben Kingsley played Othello and David Suchet, Iago.

  Iago's attitude towards women is clear from his comments about and relationship with Emilia. Some critics have pointed to evidence of a 'woman hating' attitude, which has given evidence for various theories about his motivations.

- **Feminist criticism** Feminism challenges sexism and any form of discrimination which involves the subordination of women. Feminist criticism in literature challenges the traditional presentations and interpretations of female characters. It is possible to see the three women in the play – Desdemona, Emilia and Bianca – as exploited and controlled by the men in the play. These characters can also be seen as representing women from three different social and moral hierarchies. In *Still Harping on Daughters* (1983), Lisa Jardine explores this idea by suggesting that the drama of Shakespeare's time is male-dominated and that Desdemona, ultimately, becomes a passive victim of her own attempts to be independent and challenge male dominance.

In more recent years, the focus of literary criticism has changed. Critics have largely ceased to look on characters as real people with independent lives and freedom of action. The popular approach today is to view characters as the writer's constructs, presented in particular ways to achieve particular effects.

The characters

OTHELLO, a noble Moor, General in the Venetian army

DESDEMONA, Othello's wife

CASSIO, Othello's Lieutenant

IAGO, Othello's Ancient

EMILIA, Iago's wife

RODERIGO, a Venetian gentleman, in love with Desdemona

BIANCA, a courtesan, Cassio's mistress

DUKE OF VENICE

BRABANTIO, a Venetian senator, Desdemona's father

GRATIANO, a Venetian nobleman, Brabantio's brother

LODOVICO, a Venetian nobleman, Brabantio's kinsman

FIRST SENATOR

SECOND SENATOR

MONTANO, Governor of Cyprus

FIRST GENTLEMAN

SECOND GENTLEMAN

THIRD GENTLEMAN

AN OFFICER

A SAILOR

A MESSENGER

A HERALD

A CLOWN, in Othello's household

FIRST MUSICIAN

Other SENATORS, other OFFICERS, other MUSICIANS, ATTENDANTS and SERVANTS

1:1

Roderigo angrily accuses Iago of accepting money from him without fulfilling his side of their bargain. Also, Iago is bitter about being passed over for promotion as Othello's lieutenant. Iago has a low opinion of Cassio, the man who has been given the post. Iago is set on revenge but will pretend to be a faithful servant to Othello for his own ends. Iago and Roderigo shout outside Brabantio's house, telling him that he has been 'robbed' of his daughter by Othello.

1	*Tush, never tell me* you're not seriously telling me that
2–3	*who … thine* who has controlled my money as you wished
4	*'Sblood* by God's blood

The play opens in a street in Venice in the middle of a conversation between Iago and Roderigo. It is night. The men in the street can see Brabantio but they do not want to be seen. Where would you have his window and how would it be lit? Where would Iago and Roderigo stand?

10	*In personal suit* personally appealed
11	*Off-capped* removed their hats as a sign of respect
12	*I know … place* I know what I am worth and I am worthy of the position
13	*as loving … purposes* he is full of himself and his own ideas
14–15	*Evades … war* He doesn't give them a direct answer but puts them off with long-winded excuses full of military jargon.
15	*stuffed* 'Bombast' was originally cotton used for stuffing quilts and clothes.
16	*Non-suits* rejects (the request). *mediators* supporters. *Certes* certainly
19	*Forsooth* truly (used here sarcastically). *a great arithmetician* Iago sneeringly dismisses Cassio as one who understands the theory of war but has no practical experience.
20	*a Florentine* a person from Florence (Used here sneeringly. Florence was noted as a city of culture and sophistication as opposed to the practical trade and industry of Venice.)
21	*almost … wife* This may suggest that Cassio has a liking for beautiful women.
22–3	*never … knows* never commanded a military unit in battle nor knows how to deploy troops in battle
24	*unless the bookish theoric* except in theory learned from books
26–7	*Mere … soldiership* he only knows about the skills of soldiering from talk
27	*had th' election* was chosen for promotion
28–30	*And I … be-leed and calmed* and I am passed over for promotion (a nautical reference to the lee-side – out of the wind and becalmed)
31	*'Debitor … counter-caster* Iago sees Cassio as little better than a book-keeper.
32	*Lieutenant* deputy
33	*Ancient* ensign or senior officer
36–8	*Preferment … the first* promotion is now gained by academic qualification and favouritism rather than the old method of step-by-step promotion on the basis of seniority
39	*affined* obliged
40	*Moor* Black African
42	*serve my turn upon him* use him to get what I want

1:1   *Enter* IAGO *and* RODERIGO

RODERIGO   Tush, never tell me. I take it much unkindly
            That thou, Iago, who hast had my purse
            As if the strings were thine, shouldst know of this.

IAGO   'Sblood, but you will not hear me!
            If ever I did dream of such a matter,   5
            Abhor me.

RODERIGO   Thou toldst me thou didst hold him in thy hate.

IAGO   Despise me if I do not.
            Three great ones of the city,
            In personal suit to make me his Lieutenant,   10
            Off-capped to him – and by the faith of man
            I know my price, I am worth no worse a place –
            But he, as loving his own pride and purposes,
            Evades them with a bombast circumstance
            Horribly stuffed with epithets of war;   15
            Non-suits my mediators. For, 'Certes,' says he,
            'I have already chose my officer.'
            And what was he?
            Forsooth, a great arithmetician,
            One Michael Cassio, a Florentine –   20
            A fellow almost damned in a fair wife –
            That never set a squadron in the field,
            Nor the division of a battle knows
            More than a spinster – unless the bookish theoric,
            Wherein the toga'd consuls can propose   25
            As masterly as he. Mere prattle without practice
            Is all his soldiership. But he, sir, had th'election;
            And I, of whom his eyes had seen the proof
            At Rhodes, at Cyprus, and on other grounds
            Christian and heathen, must be be-leed and calmed   30
            By 'Debitor and Creditor'. This counter-caster,
            He – in good time! – must his Lieutenant be,
            And I – God bless the mark! – his Moorship's Ancient.

RODERIGO   By heaven, I rather would have been his hangman.

IAGO   Why, there's no remedy. 'Tis the curse of service.   35
            Preferment goes by letter and affection,
            And not by old gradation, where each second
            Stood heir to the first. Now sir, be judge yourself
            Whether I in any just term am affined
            To love the Moor!

RODERIGO   I would not follow him then.   40

IAGO   Oh, sir, content you.
            I follow him to serve my turn upon him.

45   *duteous … knave* a servant who humbly serves his master

46   *doting … bondage* loves the humble and creeping life he is bound to

47   *Wears out his time* spends his life

48   *cashiered* sacked

50   *trimmed … duty* are careful to appear dutiful

51–3   *Keep … by them* look after themselves first and only appear to serve their masters

53   *lined their coats* made money for themselves

54   *Do themselves homage* serve their own interests
     soul spirit

59–60   *not I … peculiar end* I am not following him out of friendship or duty but to serve my personal interests

62   *The native act … heart* my true action actions and character

63   *In complement extern* outward behaviour

64   *I will … sleeve* openly show my real feelings

65   *for daws to peck at* for any fool to take advantage of ('daws' short for jackdaws)
     I am not what I am I am not what I appear to be

*When Iago says **I am not what I am**, he touches upon a key aspect of his character and behaviour throughout the play. Why do you think these words are important? How might an actor deliver these lines to make them as effective as possible? Would he speak them to himself? To Roderigo? To the audience?*

66   *full* good
     thick-lips offensive reference to Othello's racial feature
     owe own

67   *carry it* succeed, carry it off

It is Iago who instigates the rousing of Brabantio, but he engineers it so that it appears to be Roderigo who is taking the lead. How would you present the relationship between Iago and Roderigo here? Would you show Iago very much in command or would you show him leading Roderigo in a more subtle way? Would you present Roderigo as a fool, or as a character who is a taken in by Iago's skilful manipulation?

69   *Proclaim* denounce

70–1   *though he … flies* although his life might be pleasant now, we will plague him

72–3   *chances … colour* present the probability of trouble so that his happiness will be spoilt

75   *timorous* causing fear, terrifying

We cannot all be masters, nor all masters
Cannot be truly followed. You shall mark
Many a duteous and knee-crooking knave   45
That, doting on his own obsequious bondage,
Wears out his time, much like his master's ass,
For naught but provender, and when he's old – cashiered.
Whip me such honest knaves! Others there are
Who, trimmed in forms and visages of duty,   50
Keep yet their hearts attending on themselves,
And throwing but shows of service on their lords
Do well thrive by them; and when they have lined their coats
Do themselves homage. These fellows have some soul,
And such a one do I profess myself. For, sir,   55
It is as sure as you are Roderigo,
Were I the Moor, I would not be Iago:
In following him, I follow but myself.
Heaven is my judge, not I for love and duty,
But seeming so for my peculiar end.   60
For when my outward action doth demonstrate
The native act and figure of my heart
In complement extern, 'tis not long after
But I will wear my heart upon my sleeve
For daws to peck at: I am not what I am.   65

RODERIGO   What a full fortune does the thick-lips owe
If he can carry it thus!

IAGO   Call up her father.
Rouse him, make after him, poison his delight,
Proclaim him in the streets. Incense her kinsmen,
And though he in a fertile climate dwell,   70
Plague him with flies. Though that his joy be joy,
Yet throw such chances of vexation on't
As it may lose some colour.

RODERIGO   Here is her father's house – I'll call aloud.

IAGO   Do, with like timorous accent and dire yell   75
As when, by night and negligence, the fire
Is spied in populous cities.

RODERIGO   What, ho, Brabantio! Signor Brabantio, ho!

IAGO   Awake! What, ho, Brabantio! Thieves, thieves!
Look to your house, your daughter, and your bags!   80
Thieves, thieves!

Enter BRABANTIO, *above*

BRABANTIO   What is the reason for this terrible summons?
What is the matter there?

RODERIGO   Signor, is all your family within?

23

| | It is important here that Brabantio does not recognise Iago, even though he is doing most of the shouting. How could this be staged so that Iago's identity is not revealed? |

86	*Zounds* by God's wounds
87	*lost half your soul* has lost half of what you live for
	burst broken
88	*old black ram* insulting term for Othello
89	*tupping* the term used to describe a ram mating with a ewe
	white ewe Desdemona
90	*snorting* snoring
91	*devil* Othello – the devil was depicted as black
	make a grandsire of you make you a grandfather

| | Note that Iago's language here is powerful in provoking Brabantio. The unpleasant sexual imagery with its sordid connotations is carefully calculated to manipulate Brabantio's emotional response. Which words would Iago stress? |

94	*reverend* respected
97	*charged* ordered
99	*My daughter is not for thee* you are not going to marry my daughter
100	*distempering draughts* drinks that have disturbed and intoxicated
102	*start* disturb
104–5	*My spirits … to thee* my feelings towards you and the influence I possess have the power to make you regret this
107	*grange* a country house

| | Notice that there is a shift here from verse to prose. Why do you think this is? What effect do you think it has on the tone of Iago's speech? |

109–10	*will not serve God, if the devil bid you* foolishly refuse to do the right thing if you are advised to do it by someone you distrust
111	*covered with* mated with
	Barbary horse a breed of horse from North Africa (another reference to Othello's background)
112	*coursers* a fast horse or charges
113	*jennets* small Spanish horses
	germans blood relations
116	*making the beast with two backs* having sex (note the unpleasant connotations Iago gives it)
117	*You are a senator* perhaps a sarcastic response from Iago in response to Brabantio's Thou art a villain
118	*thou* i.e. Rodergio
	answer be called upon to explain

IAGO	Are your doors locked?	
BRABANTIO	Why, wherefore ask you this?	**85**

IAGO   Zounds, sir, you're robbed! For shame, put on your gown.
Your heart is burst, you have lost half your soul.
Even now, now, very now, an old black ram
Is tupping your white ewe. Arise, arise!
Awake the snorting citizens with the bell,   **90**
Or else the devil will make a grandsire of you.
Arise, I say!

BRABANTIO   What, have you lost your wits?

RODERIGO   Most reverend signor, do you know my voice?

BRABANTIO   Not I. What are you?   **95**

RODERIGO   My name is Roderigo.

BRABANTIO   The worser welcome:
I have charged thee not to haunt about my doors.
In honest plainness thou hast heard me say
My daughter is not for thee; and now in madness –
Being full of supper and distempering draughts –   **100**
Upon malicious knavery dost thou come
To start my quiet.

RODERIGO   Sir, sir, sir –

BRABANTIO   But thou must needs be sure
My spirits and my place have in their power
To make this bitter to thee.

RODERIGO   Patience, good sir.   **105**

BRABANTIO   What tell'st thou me of robbing? This is Venice;
My house is not a grange.

RODERIGO   Most grave Brabantio,
In simple and pure soul I come to you –

IAGO   Zounds, sir, you are one of those that will not serve God, if the
devil bid you! Because we come to do you service, and you think we are   **110**
ruffians, you'll have your daughter covered with a Barbary horse – you'll
have your nephews neigh to you, you'll have coursers for cousins, and
jennets for germans.

BRABANTIO   What profane wretch art thou?

IAGO   I am one, sir, that comes to tell you your daughter and the Moor are   **115**
making the beast with two backs.

BRABANTIO   Thou art a villain.

IAGO   You are a senator.

BRABANTIO   This thou shalt answer. I know thee, Roderigo.

RODERIGO   Sir, I will answer anything. But I beseech you –
If't be your pleasure, and most wise consent,   **120**

122   *odd-even … watch o' th' night*   early hours of the morning

124   *knave*   servant

125   *the gross clasps of a lascivious Moor*   the foul embraces of a lecherous black man

126   *your allowance*   done with your consent

127   *saucy*   insolent, impertinent

128   *manners*   sense of what is 'correct' behaviour

130   *from the sense of all civility*   contrary to good manners

131   *play and trifle with your reverence*   be disrespectful to you

134–6   *Tying her duty … everywhere*   putting everything she owns into a wandering opportunistic vagrant

136   *Straight*   straight away

139   *Strike on the tinder*   to create a light

140   *taper*   candle

141   *accident*   occurrence

143   *Farewell*   Iago does not want to be recognised.

144   *meet*   fitting
       wholesome to my place   not healthy to my position

145   *produced*   brought in as a witness

147   *gall*   make sore by chafing

148   *cast*   dismiss

149   *with such loud reason*   for such obvious reasons

150   *stands in act*   the action has already begun

151–2   *Another … business*   they have no one of his ability to lead their army

157   *Saggitary*   the inn or lodging where Desdemona and Othello are staying
       raisèd search   the search party led by Roderigo

160   *despisèd time*   Brabantio feels that his life has been dishonoured by Desdemona's behaviour

As partly I find it is, that your fair daughter –
At this odd-even and dull watch o' th' night
Transported with no worse nor better guard
But with a knave of common hire, a gondolier,
To the gross clasps of a lascivious Moor –   **125**
If this be known to you, and your allowance,
We then have done you bold and saucy wrongs;
But if you know not this, my manners tell me
We have your wrong rebuke. Do not believe
That from the sense of all civility   **130**
I thus would play and trifle with your reverence.
Your daughter – if you have not given her leave,
I say again – hath made a gross revolt,
Tying her duty, beauty, wit and fortunes
In an extravagant and wheeling stranger   **135**
Of here and everywhere. Straight satisfy yourself:
If she be in her chamber, or your house,
Let loose on me the justice of the state
For thus deluding you.

BRABANTIO   Strike on the tinder, ho!
Give me a taper. Call up all my people!   **140**
This accident is not unlike my dream –
Belief of it oppresses me already.
Light, I say! Light!

                                                          [*Exit*

IAGO   Farewell for I must leave you.
It seems not meet, nor wholesome to my place,
To be produced – as if I stay I shall –   **145**
Against the Moor. For I do know the state,
However this may gall him with some check,
Cannot with safety cast him: he's embarked
With such loud reason to the Cyprus wars,
Which even now stands in act, that for their souls   **150**
Another of his fathom they have none
To lead their business. In which regard,
Though I do hate him as I do hell pains,
Yet for necessity of present life
I must show out a flag and sign of love,   **155**
Which is indeed but sign. That you shall surely find him,
Lead to the Sagittary the raisèd search,
And there will I be with him. So farewell.

                                                          [*Exit*

          Enter **BRABANTIO** *with* **SERVANTS** *and torches*

BRABANTIO   It is too true an evil. Gone she is,
And what's to come of my despisèd time   **160**

27

165   *Past thought* her behaviour is beyond imagining
       tapers lights

168   *treason of the blood* rebellion of daughter against father
       (suggesting this is an unnatural act)

170   *charms* magic charms or love potions (the first of many
       suggestions that Othello has used witchcraft to seduce
       Desdemona)

171   *property* true nature

174   *O would … had her!* I wish you had married her (Brabantio has
       changed his mind about Roderigo. See lines 96–7.)

175   *Some one way … another* The search parties go off in different
       directions.

182   *deserve your pains* I will reward you for your trouble

---

Compare the impression given of Othello by Iago in this scene with the
impression that is created when he actually appears in the next scene. Make a
note of any key differences. What do any differences tell you about
(a) Othello; (b) Iago; (c) Shakespeare's purpose?

Compare Iago's reasons for hating Othello given in this scene with those he
gives at the end of Act 3 Scene 3. What do you think of his reasons?

---

*Iago has revealed (a) his own hatred of Othello and has persuaded Roderigo to rouse
Brabantio and tell him is daughter has secretly married Othello, and (b) his hatred
for Cassio who has been promoted to Othello's lieutenant, a position Iago sees as
rightfully his. Outwardly though, he pretends to be loyal and faithful to Othello.*

1:2

*Iago, pretending to be loyal to Othello, tells him about Brabantio's response to
news of his elopement. Cassio arrives summoning Othello to attend the Senate
on urgent business and then Brabantio arrives, and wants Othello arrested. They
all go to the Senate to see the Duke and senators.*

1   *in the trade of war* carrying out my job as a soldier

2   *very stuff o' th' conscience* fundamental to honest behaviour

3   *contrived* planned beforehand

3–4   *I lack … service* I lack the unscrupulous nature needed to
       advance myself

5   *yerked* stabbed

7   *scurvy* unpleasant

10   *I did … him* I had great difficulty stopping myself from attacking him

11   *fast* definitely

Is naught but bitterness. Now, Roderigo,
Where didst thou see her? – Oh unhappy girl! –
With the Moor, say'st thou? – Who would be a father? –
How didst thou know 'twas she? – Oh, she deceives me
Past thought! – What said she to you? Get more tapers.   165
Raise all my kindred. – Are they married, think you?

RODERIGO   Truly I think they are.

BRABANTIO   Oh heaven! How got she out? Oh treason of the blood!
Fathers, from hence trust not your daughters' minds
By what you see them act. Is there not charms   170
By which the property of youth and maidhood
May be abused? Have you not read, Roderigo,
Of some such thing?

RODERIGO   Yes, sir, I have indeed.

BRABANTIO   Call up my brother. – Oh would you had had her! –
Some one way, some another. – Do you know   175
Where we may apprehend her and the Moor?

RODERIGO   I think I can discover him, if you please
To get good guard and go along with me.

BRABANTIO   Pray you lead on. At every house I'll call;
I may command at most. – Get weapons, ho!   180
And raise some special officers of night. –
On, good Roderigo, I will deserve your pains.

                                                    [*Exeunt*

1:2   Enter **OTHELLO**, **IAGO**, *and* ATTENDANTS *with torches*

IAGO   Though in the trade of war I have slain men,
Yet do I hold it very stuff o' th' conscience
To do no contrived murder: I lack iniquity
Sometime to do me service. Nine or ten times
I had thought to have yerked him here under the ribs.   5

OTHELLO   'Tis better as it is.

IAGO   Nay, but he prated
And spoke such scurvy and provoking terms
Against your honour,
That, with the little godliness I have,
I did full hard forbear him. But I pray you, sir,   10
Are you fast married? Be assured of this,

12   *the magnifico* an important man, i.e. Brabantio

13–14   *hath … Duke's* almost as powerful as the Duke

15–17   *Or put … cable* impose whatever restraint can be applied under the law

> We see Othello for the first time here. What kind of impression might an actor want to make of Othello on his first entrance? How might he be dressed? In civilian clothes? Fashionable clothes? Military uniform? Ethnic costume? What kind of tone might he use to speak lines 17–28?

Ben Kingsley as Othello in RSC 1985 production

18   *Signory* the Venetian government

19   *out-tongue* put forward a stronger argument
       'Tis yet to know yet to be made known

21   *promulgate* make known

22–4   *my demerits … have reached* my merits will modestly show that my status is as high as that of the family he has married into

25–8   *But that … seas' worth* if I did not love Desdemona I would not restrict or confine my freedom for all the treasure in the sea

31   *parts* personal qualities
       title legal rights through marriage
       perfect soul clear conscience

32   *manifest me rightly* make it clear that I am in the right

33   *Janus* Roman god with two faces – an appropriate god for Iago to swear by

37   *haste-post-haste* as quickly as possible

39   *divine* understand

40   *heat* urgency

41   *sequent* one after another

44   *hotly* urgently

46   *about* all around the city
       several separate

That the magnifico is much beloved,
And hath in his effect a voice potential
As double as the Duke's. He will divorce you,
Or put upon you what restraint or grievance   15
The law – with all his might to enforce it on –
Will give him cable.

OTHELLO   Let him do his spite.
My services, which I have done the Signory,
Shall out-tongue his complaints. 'Tis yet to know –
Which, when I know that boasting is an honour,   20
I shall promulgate – I fetch my life and being
From men of royal siege; and my demerits
May speak unbonneted to as proud a fortune
As this that I have reached. For know, Iago,
But that I love the gentle Desdemona,   25
I would not my unhousèd free condition
Put into circumscription and confine
For the seas' worth. But look, what lights come yond?

Enter **CASSIO** *with* **OFFICERS** *and torches*

IAGO   Those are the raisèd father and his friends.
You were best go in.

OTHELLO   Not I. I must be found.   30
My parts, my title, and my perfect soul
Shall manifest me rightly. Is it they?

IAGO   By Janus, I think no.

OTHELLO   The servants of the Duke? And my Lieutenant?
The goodness of the night upon you, friends!   35
What is the news?

CASSIO   The Duke does greet you, General,
And he requires your haste-post-haste appearance
Even on the instant.

OTHELLO   What is the matter, think you?

CASSIO   Something from Cyprus, as I may divine;
It is a business of some heat. The galleys   40
Have sent a dozen sequent messengers
This very night at one another's heels,
And many of the consuls, raised and met,
Are at the Duke's already. You have been hotly called for.
When being not at your lodging to be found,   45
The Senate hath sent about three several quests
To search you out.

OTHELLO   'Tis well I am found by you.
I will but spend a word here in the house
And go with you.

                                        [*Exit*

49   *what makes he here?* what is he doing?

50   *boarded a land carrack* taken as a prize, a treasure-ship (i.e. Othello has taken a wealthy woman as his wife.)

51   *lawful prize* if their marriage is lawful

52   *I do not understand* We later learn that Cassio helped Othello in his courtship of Desdemona. He is loyally keeping Othello's secret here.

53   *Have with you* I'll come with you

> How might the actors playing Brabantio and Othello present this confrontation? How could the contrast between them be emphasised on stage? How do you imagine Othello speaking lines 59–61? Suggest some actions or movements Othello and Brabantio could make here.

55   *be advised* be careful

58   *I am for you* I will fight you (Iago here makes a pretence of attacking Roderigo.)

59   *Keep … rust them* This shows Othello's calm authority.

60   *you shall … with years* you will command more respect due to your age than weapons

62   *stowed* hidden away

63   *thou hast enchanted her* you have put a spell on her

64   *I'll refer … sense* according to common sense

67   *opposite* opposed

68   *wealthy … nation* rich young noblemen with their fashionable curled hair

69   *to incur a general mock* to be a public laughing stock

70   *guardage* from my protection
     sooty another reference to Othello's colour

71   *to fear, not to delight* Brabantio cannot understand how Desdemona can find happiness with a black man.

72   *Judge … in sense* I ask the world to judge whether it isn't completely obvious

73   *practised … charms* used unpleasant methods to trick and deceive her

74   *minerals* drugs or poisons

75   *weakens motion* weakens her resistance
     disputed argued in court

76   *palpable* obvious

77   *attach* arrest

78   *abuser* deceiver or corrupter

79   *arts … warrant* forbidden or illegal practices (i.e. witchcraft and the 'black' arts)

Cassio	Ancient, what makes he here?
Iago	Faith, he tonight hath boarded a land carrack; 50
	If it prove lawful prize, he's made for ever.
Cassio	I do not understand.
Iago	He's married.
Cassio	To who?

Enter **Othello**

Iago	Marry, to – Come, Captain, will you go?
Othello	Have with you.
Cassio	Here comes another troop to seek for you.

Enter **Brabantio**, **Roderigo**, *with* **officers** *and torches*

Iago	It is Brabantio. General, be advised; 55
	He comes to bad intent.
Othello	Holla! Stand there.
Roderigo	Signor, it is the Moor.
Brabantio	Down with him thief!
Iago	You, Roderigo? Come sir, I am for you.
Othello	Keep up your bright swords, for the dew will rust them.
	Good signor, you shall more command with years 60
	Than with your weapons.
Brabantio	Oh thou foul thief! Where hast thou stowed my daughter?
	Damned as thou art, thou hast enchanted her.
	For I'll refer me to all things of sense,
	If she in chains of magic were not bound, 65
	Whether a maid, so tender, fair and happy,
	So opposite to marriage that she shunned
	The wealthy curlèd darlings of our nation,
	Would ever have – to incur a general mock –
	Run from her guardage to the sooty bosom 70
	Of such a thing as thou – to fear, not to delight.
	Judge me the world, if 'tis not gross in sense
	That thou hast practised on her with foul charms,
	Abused her delicate youth with drugs or minerals
	That weakens motion. I'll have 't disputed on; 75
	'Tis probable, and palpable to thinking.
	I therefore apprehend and do attach thee
	For an abuser of the world, a practiser
	Of arts inhibited and out of warrant.
	Lay hold upon him. If he do resist, 80
	Subdue him at his peril.
Othello	Hold your hands,
	Both you of my inclining and the rest.

Brabantio makes a long speech accusing Othello (lines 62–81). Othello does not interrupt him. How does he react whilst Brabantio is speaking? What kind of facial expression might he have? What kind of body language does he show?

82   *you of my inclining* my supporters
86   *course of direct session* immediate trial
95   *idle cause* trivial claim
96   *my brothers of state* fellow senators
98   *if such … passage face* if people are allowed to get away with such actions
99   *Bond-slaves and pagans* slaves and heathens (another insulting reference to Othello's background)

How does the impression you gain of Othello in this scene compare with the picture Iago paints of him in Scene 1?

Things develop as Iago had hoped and Brabatio confronts Othello. Othello is called by the Duke to the Senate on urgent business. Brabantio goes too to voice his complaints about Othello to the Duke and senators.

1:3

Reports are coming in about an imminent Turkish attack on Cyprus. The Duke listens to Brabantio's complaint and then Othello gives his version of events which Desdemona verifies. Othello is sent as Governor of Cyprus to defend the island. Iago comes up with the idea of using Cassio to make Othello jealous.

1   *composition* consistency, sense
2   *gives them credit* makes them believable
     disproportioned inconsistent
5   *jump … accompt* do not agree on an exact number
6   *the aim reports* the report is based on an estimated number
10 *I do not … error* I do not find comfort in these inconsistencies
11 *But … approve* I accept the general information in the reports
12 *fearful sense* with a sense of fear

Were it my cue to fight, I should have known it
Without a prompter. Where will you that I go
To answer this your charge?

BRABANTIO   To prison, till fit time   **85**
Of law and course of direct session
Call thee to answer.

OTHELLO   What if I do obey?
How may the Duke be therewith satisfied,
Whose messengers are here about my side
Upon some present business of the state   **90**
To bring me to him?

OFFICER   'Tis true, most worthy signor;
The Duke's in council, and your noble self
I am sure is sent for.

BRABANTIO   How? The Duke in council?
In this time of the night? Bring him away.
Mine's not an idle cause: The Duke himself,   **95**
Or any of my brothers of the state,
Cannot but feel this wrong as 'twere their own.
For if such actions may have passage free,
Bond-slaves and pagans shall our statesmen be.

[*Exeunt*

1:3   *Enter* DUKE *and* SENATORS, *who sit at a table, with* OFFICERS *and lights*

DUKE   There is no composition in these news
That gives them credit.

FIRST SENATOR   Indeed, they are disproportioned;
My letters say a hundred and seven galleys.

DUKE   And mine a hundred forty.

SECOND SENATOR   And mine two hundred.
But though they jump not on a just accompt –   **5**
As in these cases where the aim reports
'Tis oft with difference – yet do they all confirm
A Turkish fleet, and bearing up to Cyprus.

DUKE   Nay, it is possible enough to judgement.
I do not so secure me in the error   **10**
But the main article I do approve
In fearful sense.

> *What impression might be created on stage at the opening of this scene? What would be the setting? A library? An operations room? An ornate hall? How might the Duke and senators be dressed? What could their reaction be to the news from the messengers? How could the actors' facial expressions and movements convey a sense of this mood?*

14	*The Turkish … Rhodes* the Turkish fleet is heading towards Rhodes
17	*How … change* what do you have to say about this change (i.e. that the fleet is now heading towards Rhodes rather than Cyprus)
18	*no assay of reason* test of reason *pageant* deceptive show
19	*keep … gaze* keep us looking in the wrong direction
20	*importancy* importance
22	*as it … Rhodes* Cyprus is more important to the Turks than Rhodes
23	*so … bear it* so the Turks can capture it with less struggle
24	*it stands … brace* it is not so well fortified
25–6	*lacks … dressed in* lacks the ability to defend itself as well as Rhodes
29–30	*Neglecting … profitless* giving up a chance to make an easy gain in order to take risks for no profit
31	*in all confidence* I am sure
33	*Ottomites* Turks *revered and gracious* The messenger respectfully addresses the Duke and Senate.
35	*injointed…fleet* joined up with a fleet sailing after them
37–8	*re-stem … course* turn back on to their original course
38–9	*bearing … Cyprus* openly heading towards Cyprus
40	*servitor* servant
41	*With his … thus* respectfully offers this information

> *How does the Duke welcome (a) Othello and (b) Brabantio? What does this tell you about how he views each of them in the current crisis?*

SAILOR [*Within*]   What, ho! What, ho! What, ho!

Enter a SAILOR

OFFICER   A messenger from the galleys.

DUKE   Now, what's the business?

SAILOR   The Turkish preparation makes for Rhodes.
  So was I bid report here to the state   **15**
  By Signor Angelo.

DUKE   How say you by this change?

FIRST SENATOR   This cannot be,
  By no assay of reason. 'Tis a pageant
  To keep us in false gaze. When we consider
  The importancy of Cyprus to the Turk,   **20**
  And let ourselves again but understand
  That, as it more concerns the Turk than Rhodes,
  So may he with more facile question bear it,
  For that it stands not in such warlike brace,
  But altogether lacks the abilities   **25**
  That Rhodes is dressed in – if we make thought of this,
  We must not think the Turk is so unskilful
  To leave that latest which concerns him first,
  Neglecting an attempt of ease and gain
  To wake and wage a danger profitless.   **30**

DUKE   Nay, in all confidence he's not for Rhodes.

OFFICER   Here is more news.

Enter a MESSENGER

MESSENGER   The Ottomites, reverend and gracious,
  Steering with due course toward the isle of Rhodes,
  Have there injointed them with an after fleet.   **35**

FIRST SENATOR Ay, so I thought! How many, as you guess?

MESSENGER   Of thirty sail, and now they do re-stem
  Their backward course, bearing with frank appearance
  Their purposes toward Cyprus. Signor Montano,
  Your trusty and most valiant servitor,   **40**
  With his free duty recommends you thus,
  And prays you to believe him.

DUKE   'Tis certain then for Cyprus.
  Marcus Luccicos, is not he in town?

FIRST SENATOR He's now in Florence.   **45**

DUKE   Write from us to him; post-post-haste dispatch.

FIRST SENATOR Here comes Brabantio and the valiant Moor.

Enter BRABANTIO, OTHELLO, CASSIO, IAGO, RODERIGO, *and* OFFICERS

48	*straight* immediately
49	*general enemy* public enemy
	Ottoman Turkish
53–4	*Neither … bed* it wasn't anything to do with my official position nor any news of public affairs which made me leave my bed
54	*general care* public concern
56–8	*Is of so … still itself* is like a flood, so overwhelming that it pushes everything else aside and yet still continues
61	*mountebanks* fake doctors
62	*For nature … err* nature couldn't go so wrong
63	*Being not deficient … sense* not being blind or stupid
64	*Sans witchcraft could not* could not have happened without witchcraft
65	*Whoe'er he be* whoever he is
	in this foul proceeding by these foul means
66	*Hath … herself* has lured your daughter away against her own nature
67	*the bloody book of law* the vengeance prescribed by law
68	*You … letter* you shall implement to the letter
69–70	*though … action* even if my own son were the one accused
72	*mandate* command

How does Othello handle the situation in lines 76–94? What would be the key impression that you would want to give the audience here if you were playing the role of Othello?

76	*potent* powerful
80–1	*The very … extent* this is the full extent of my offence
81	*Rude* simple
83	*For since … pith* since the age of seven
	pith strength
84	*Till now … wasted* until nine months ago
84–5	*they have … field* they have most on the field in battle

DUKE Valiant Othello, we must straight employ you
   Against the general enemy Ottoman.
   [*To* BRABANTIO] I did not see you; welcome, gentle signor.   **50**
   We lacked your counsel and your help tonight.

BRABANTIO So did I yours. Good your grace, pardon me:
   Neither my place, nor aught I heard of business,
   Hath raised me from my bed; nor doth the general care
   Take hold on me, for my particular grief   **55**
   Is of so flood-gate and o'erbearing nature
   That it engluts and swallows other sorrows,
   And it is still itself.

DUKE   Why, what's the matter?

BRABANTIO My daughter! Oh my daughter!

SENATORS   Dead?

BRABANTIO   Ay, to me.
   She is abused, stol'n from me, and corrupted   **60**
   By spells and medicines bought of mountebanks;
   For nature so preposterously to err,
   Being not deficient, blind, or lame of sense,
   Sans witchcraft could not.

DUKE Whoe'er he be that in this foul proceeding   **65**
   Hath thus beguiled your daughter of herself,
   And you of her, the bloody book of law
   You shall yourself read, in the bitter letter,
   After its own sense – yea, though our proper son
   Stood in your action.

BRABANTIO   Humbly I thank your grace.   **70**
   Here is the man: this Moor, whom now it seems
   Your special mandate, for the state affairs,
   Hath hither brought.

SENATORS   We are very sorry for't.

DUKE [*To* OTHELLO] What in your own part can you say to this?

BRABANTIO Nothing, but this is so.   **75**

OTHELLO Most potent, grave and reverend signors,
   My very noble and approved good masters:
   That I have ta'en away this old man's daughter,
   It is most true; true I have married her;
   The very head and front of my offending   **80**
   Hath this extent, no more. Rude am I in my speech,
   And little blessed with the soft phrase of peace;
   For since these arms of mine had seven years' pith,
   Till now, some nine moons wasted, they have used
   Their dearest action in the tented field;   **85**
   And little of this great world can I speak

87   *pertains* relates
       broils fights

88   *grace my cause* improve my case

90   *round* to the point
       unvarnished plain

92   *conjuration* spells

94   *bold* immodest

95–6   *her motion…herself* she was so shy she even blushed at her own emotions

96   *nature* natural character

97   *credit* reputation

99–101   *It is … nature* only someone with poor judgement could believe that someone as perfect as Desdemona could go against her nature

103   *vouch* assert, state

104   *mixtures* potions

105   *dram conjured* drug prepared with magic

106   *wrought upon her* cast a spell on her
       To vouch…proof to assert this does not prove it

107   *Overt* open, obvious

108   *thin habits* suspect ideas
       poor likelihoods unlikely conclusions

109   *modern seeming* ordinary events
       prefer against him offer evidence against him

111   *indirect and forcèd courses* cunning and devious actions

113   *question* discussions

117   *find … report* gives a bad report of me

123   *blood* nature, character

More than pertains to feats of broils and battle;
And therefore little shall I grace my cause
In speaking for myself. Yet, by your gracious patience,
I will a round unvarnished tale deliver   90
Of my whole course of love: what drugs, what charms,
What conjuration, and what mighty magic –
For such proceeding I am charged withal –
I won his daughter.

BRABANTIO   A maiden never bold,
    Of spirit so still and quiet that her motion   95
    Blushed at herself – and she, in spite of nature,
    Of years, of country, credit, everything,
    To fall in love with what she feared to look on!
    It is a judgement maimed and most imperfect
    That will confess perfection so could err   100
    Against all rules of nature, and must be driven
    To find out practices of cunning hell
    Why this should be. I therefore vouch again
    That with some mixtures powerful o'er the blood,
    Or with some dram conjured to this effect,   105
    He wrought upon her.

DUKE   To vouch this is no proof
    Without more wider and more overt test
    Than these thin habits and poor likelihoods
    Of modern seeming do prefer against him.

FIRST SENATOR But Othello, speak –   110
    Did you by indirect and forcèd courses
    Subdue and poison this young maid's affections?
    Or came it by request, and such fair question
    As soul to soul affordeth?

OTHELLO   I do beseech you,
    Send for the lady to the Sagittary,   115
    And let her speak of me before her father;
    If you do find me foul in her report,
    The trust, the office, I do hold of you
    Not only take away, but let your sentence
    Even fall upon my life.

DUKE   Fetch Desdemona hither.   120

OTHELLO   Ancient, conduct them: you best know the place.

                        [Exeunt IAGO *and two or three* OFFICERS

And till she come, as truly as to heaven
I do confess the vices of my blood,
So justly to your grave ears I'll present
How I did thrive in this fair lady's love,   125

128 *Still* continually

133 *chances* chance happenings

134 *moving accidents … field* exciting events on sea and land

135 *hair-breadth scapes* narrow escapes

137 *redemption* freed after payment of a ransom

138 *portance* behaviour

139 *antres* caves
idle empty

141 *hint* occasion
process story

143 *Anthropophagi* cannibals

145 *seriously incline* lean forward listening intently

146 *still* always

149 *discourse* conversation

150 *pliant* convenient

152 *all my pilgrimage dilate* give a full account of all my travels

153 *by parcels* in bits and pieces

154 *intentively* paying full attention

155 *did beguile … tears* caused her to cry

156 *stroke* blow

158 *pains* sufferings

159 *passing* extremely

162 *had made her such a man* had made her into a man like that

How do you imagine Othello delivering his explanation in lines 127–69?
Tenderly? Humourously? Passionately? Defensively? What do you think of the
Duke's response?

	And she in mine.	
DUKE	Say it, Othello.	
OTHELLO	Her father loved me; oft invited me;	

Still questioned me the story of my life
From year to year – the battle, sieges, fortune
That I have passed.   **130**
I ran it through, even from my boyish days
To the very moment that he bade me tell it:
Wherein I spoke of most disastrous chances,
Of moving accidents by flood and field,
Of hair-breadth scapes i' th' imminent deadly breach,   **135**
Of being taken by the insolent foe
And sold to slavery, of my redemption thence,
And portance in my traveller's history;
Wherein of antres vast and deserts idle,
Rough quarries, rocks, and hills whose heads touch heaven,   **140**
It was my hint to speak – such was my process –
And of the Cannibals that each other eat,
The Anthropophagi, and men whose heads
Grew beneath their shoulders. These things to hear
Would Desdemona seriously incline;   **145**
But still the house affairs would draw here hence,
Which ever as she could with haste dispatch
She'd come again, and with a greedy ear
Devour up my discourse; which I observing
Took once a pliant hour and found good means   **150**
To draw from her a prayer of earnest heart
That I would all my pilgrimage dilate,
Whereof by parcels she had something heard,
But not intentively. I did consent,
And often did beguile her of her tears   **155**
When I did speak of some distressful stroke
That my youth suffered. My story being done,
She gave me for my pains a world of sighs;
She swore in faith 'twas strange, 'twas passing strange,
'Twas pitiful, 'twas wondrous pitiful.   **160**
She wished she had not heard it, yet she wished
That heaven had made her such a man. She thanked me,
And bade me, if I had a friend that loved her,
I should but teach him how to tell my story,
And that would woo her. Upon this hint I spake.   **165**
She loved me for the dangers I had passed,
and I loved her that she did pity them.
This only is the witchcraft I have used.
Here comes the lady. Let her witness it.

Enter **DESDEMONA**, **IAGO** *and* **OFFICERS**

171   *take up … best* make the best of this confused business

172–3   *Men do … bare hands* make the best of what you have got

180   *education* upbringing

181   *learn* teach

182   *lord of duty* the person I owe obedience to

186   *challenge* claim

189   *I had … get it* I wish I had adopted a child rather than fathered one

196   *To hang clogs on them* to hang blocks of wood on them to stop them getting away

197   *lay a sentence* make a judgement

198   *grize* first move

200–1   *When remedies … depended* when we know there is no remedy for a situation we must put the grief behind us. It is no good living in hope of an improvement

202   *mischief* disaster

205   *Patience her injury … makes* patience allows you to laugh at your injuries

206–7   *The robbed … grief* a person robbed who shows they don't care takes away some of the thief's satisfaction; you just harm yourself by indulging in pointless unhappiness

208   *beguile* cheat

210–11   *He bears … hears* a person bears a verdict well if all he hears is the comforting advice which follows it

212–13   *But he … borrow* in order to endure grief he must draw on his reserves of patience

DUKE	I think this tale would win my daughter too.	170

DUKE   I think this tale would win my daughter too. 170
Good Brabantio, take up this mangled matter at the best:
Men do their broken weapons rather use
Than their bare hands.

BRABANTIO   I pray you hear her speak.
If she confess that she was half the wooer,
Destruction on my head if my bad blame 175
Light on the man. Come hither, gentle mistress:
Do you perceive in all this noble company
Where most you owe obedience?

DESDEMONA   My noble father,
I do perceive here a divided duty.
To you I am bound for life and education; 180
My life and education both do learn me
How to respect you: you are the lord of duty –
I am hitherto your daughter. But here's my husband;
And so much duty as my mother showed
To you, preferring you before her father, 185
So much I challenge that I may profess
Due to the Moor my lord.

BRABANTIO   God be with you! I have done.
Please it your grace, on to the state affairs.
I had rather to adopt a child than get it.
Come hither, Moor: 190
I here do give thee that with all my heart
Which, but thou hast already, with all my heart
I would keep from thee. For your sake, jewel,
I am glad at soul I have no other child,
For thy escape would teach me tyranny 195
To hang clogs on them. I have done, my lord.

DUKE   Let me speak like yourself, and lay a sentence
Which as a grize or step may help these lovers
Into your favour.
When remedies are past, the griefs are ended 200
By seeing the worst, which late on hopes depended.
To mourn a mischief that is past and gone
Is the next way to draw new mischief on.
What cannot be preserved when fortune takes,
Patience her injury a mockery makes. 205
The robbed that smiles, steals something from the thief;
He robs himself that spends a bootless grief.

BRABANTIO So let the Turk of Cyprus us beguile,
We lose it not so long as we can smile.
He bears the sentence well that nothing bears 210
But the free comfort which from thence he hears;
But he bears both the sentence and the sorrow

214	*to sugar, or to gall* to sweeten or make bitter
215	*equivocal* equal
216–17	*I never yet … the ear* I've never heard yet that an emotional hurt can be made better by words
219	*preparation* fleet prepared for battle
220	*fortitude* strength (of the military defences)
221	*substitute … sufficiency* a deputy with a reputation for competence
221–2	*a sovereign mistress of effects* which finally decides what should be done
222	*throws a more safer voice on you* would feel safer with you in charge
223	*slubber* spoil
224	*stubborn* hard *boisterous* violent
225	*tyrant custom* habit
227	*thrice-driven* softest
227–9	*I do agnize … hardness* I acknowledge that I take well to harsh conditions
231	*bending to your state* bowing to your authority
232	*fit disposition* suitable arrangements
233	*Due reference of place* treatment befitting her rank *exhibition* financial provision
234	*besort* attendants
235	*As levels with her breeding* appropriate for her status
239	*my unfolding* my plan *prosperous* favourable
240	*charter* support
241	*simpleness* innocence
243	*downright … fortunes* my drastic actions taking my fortunes by storm
244–5	*My hearts … lord* I love everything about Othello's nature and character
246	*visage* face
247	*valiant parts* military qualities
248	*Did I my soul and fortunes consecrate* I dedicated my life and future to him
250	*moth* a fragile thing
251	*The rites … bereft me* I would be denied of my privileges as a wife
252	*a heavy interim shall support* I shall have to endure a difficult period

What is your impression of Desdemona? What impressions could an actress create by speaking these lines in different ways? Regretfully? Defiantly? Tenderly? Patiently? How could her movements on stage show a sense of being torn between two duties?

	That to pay grief must of poor patience borrow.
	These sentences to sugar, or to gall,
	Being strong on both sides, are equivocal.	215
	But words are words: I never yet did hear
	That the bruised heart was piercèd through the ear.
	I humbly beseech you, proceed to the affairs of state.

DUKE   The Turk with a most mighty preparation makes for Cyprus.
Othello, the fortitude of the place is best known to you; and though we   220
have there a substitute of most allowed sufficiency, yet opinion, a
sovereign mistress of effects, throws a more safer voice on you. You
must therefore be content to slubber the gloss of your new fortunes
with this more stubborn and boisterous expedition.

OTHELLO   The tyrant custom, most grave senators,   225
Hath made the flinty and steel couch of war
My thrice-driven bed of down. I do agnize
A natural and prompt alacrity
I find in hardness, and do undertake
This present war against the Ottomites.   230
Most humbly therefore, bending to your state,
I crave fit disposition for my wife,
Due reference of place and exhibition,
With such accommodation and besort
As levels with her breeding.

DUKE   Why, at her father's.   235

BRABANTIO   I will not have it so.

OTHELLO   Nor I.

DESDEMONA   Nor would I there reside,
To put my father in impatient thoughts
By being in his eye. Most gracious Duke,
To my unfolding lend your prosperous ear,
And let me find a charter in your voice   240
To assist my simpleness.

DUKE   What would you, Desdemona?

DESDEMONA That I love the Moor to live with him,
My downright violence and storm of fortunes
May trumpet to the world. My heart's subdued
Even to the very quality of my lord.   245
I saw Othello's visage in his mind,
And to his honours and his valiant parts
Did I my soul and fortunes consecrate;
So that, dear lords, if I be left behind
A moth of peace, and he go to the war,   250
The rites for why I love him are bereft me,
And I a heavy interim shall support
By his dear absence. Let me go with him.

254	*voice* consent
255	*Vouch with me* be my witness
256	*To please the palate of my appetite* to gratify my sexual desires
257	*to comply with heat* to satisfy my lust
258	*defunct* ended
259	*mind* wishes
260	*heaven defend* heaven forbid
261	*scant* neglect
262	*toys* fancies
263	*Cupid* the winged god of love
263–4	*seel … instrument* cloud my eyes with sexual desire
265	*That … business* so that such pleasure distract me from my professional work
266	*skillet* saucepan
267	*indign* unworthy
268	*Make head against my estimation* attack my reputation
270	*cries* demands
275	*commission* orders
276	*quality and respect* importance and relevance
277	*import* concern
279	*honesty* take note of this word. This is the first of many times when the word is applied to Iago. We, of course, know that he is anything but honest.
280	*conveyance* care (Iago is to look after Desdemona.)
284	*If virtue … lack* goodness is not without beauty
287–8	*Look to her … may thee* Brabantio warns Othello that Desdemona may deceive him. This is significant because of what Othello believes later.
292	*in the best advantage* when the best opportunity arises
294	*worldly matter* practical matters *direction* instructions

OTHELLO	Let her have your voice.
	Vouch with me, heaven, I therefore beg it not 255
	To please the palate of my appetite,
	Nor to comply with heat – the young affects
	In me defunct – and proper satisfaction,
	But to be free and bounteous to her mind;
	And heaven defend your good souls that you think 260
	I will your serious and great business scant
	When she is with me. No, when light-winged toys
	Of feathered Cupid seel with wanton dullness
	My speculative and officed instrument,
	That my disports corrupt and taint my business, 265
	Let housewives make a skillet of my helm,
	And all indign and base adversities
	Make head against my estimation!

DUKE   Be it as you shall privately determine,
         Either for her stay or going. The affair cries haste, 270
         And speed must answer it.

FIRST SENATOR   You must away tonight.

OTHELLO   With all my heart.

DUKE   At nine i' the' morning here we'll meet again.
         Othello, leave some officer behind,
         And he shall our commission bring to you, 275
         And such things else of quality and respect
         As doth import you.

OTHELLO   So please your grace, my Ancient –
         A man he is of honesty and trust –
         To his conveyance I assign my wife, 280
         With what else needful your good grace shall think
         To be sent after me.

DUKE   Let it be so.
         Good night to every one. And, noble signor,
         If virtue no delighted beauty lack,
         Your son-in-law is far more fair than black. 285

FIRST SENATOR Adieu, brave Moor; use Desdemona well.

BRABANTIO   Look to her, Moor, if thou hast eyes to see:
         She has deceived her father, and may thee.

                 [Exeunt **DUKE**, **BRABANTIO**, **CASSIO**, **SENATORS** *and* **OFFICERS**

OTHELLO   My life upon her faith! Honest Iago,
         My Desdemona must I leave to thee. 290
         I prithee let thy wife attend on her,
         And bring them after in the best advantage.
         Come, Desdemona, I have but an hour
         Of love, of worldly matter and direction

295 *obey the time* act according to the situation

300 *incontinently* immediately

304 *prescription* a right

307 *love himself* serve his own interests

308 *guinea-hen* a derogatory term for a woman

310 *fond* foolishly infatuated

311 *virtue* power

312 *Virtue? A fig!* I couldn't care less about virtue

314 *set* plant

315 *gender* species
distract vary

317 *corrigible authority* able to correct
beam balance

318 *poise* balance out
blood passion

320 *motions* impulses

320–1 *carnal stings* sexual desires

321 *unbitted* unrestrained

322 *sect or scion* cutting or offshoot

326 *professed me* declared myself
thy deserving your interests

327 *perdurable* everlasting
stead help

328 *defeat thy favour* disguise your face

329 *usurped* assumed

332 *answerable sequestation* corresponding separation

333 *wills* sexual desires

334 *locusts* sweet fruit

335 *coloquintida* a bitter fruit
youth a younger man

Ian McKellen as Iago in 1989 production

To spend with thee. We must obey the time.   295

[*Exeunt* OTHELLO *and* DESDEMONA

RODERIGO   Iago!

IAGO   What say'st thou, noble heart?

RODERIGO   What will I do, think'st thou?

IAGO   Why, go to bed and sleep.

RODERIGO   I will incontinently drown myself.   300

IAGO   If thou dost, I shall never love thee after.
            Why, thou silly gentleman?

RODERIGO   It is silliness to live when to live is torment; and then have we a
            prescription to die, when death is our physician.

IAGO   Oh villainous! I have looked upon the world for four times seven   305
            years, and since I could distinguish betwixt a benefit and an injury, I
            never found man that knew how to love himself. Ere I would say I
            would drown myself for the love of a guinea-hen, I would change my
            humanity with a baboon.

RODERIGO   What should I do? I confess it is my shame to be so fond, but it is   310
            not in my virtue to amend it.

IAGO   Virtue? A fig! 'Tis in ourselves that we are thus, or thus. Our
            bodies are our gardens, to the which our wills are gardeners; so that if
            we will plant nettles or sow lettuce, set hyssop and weed up thyme,
            supply it with one gender of herbs or distract it with many, either to   315
            have it sterile with idleness or manured with industry – why, the power
            and corrigible authority of this lies in our wills. If the beam of our lives
            had not one scale of reason to poise another of sensuality, the blood and
            baseness of our natures would conduct us to most preposterous
            conclusions. But we have reason to cool our raging motions, our carnal   320
            stings or unbitted lusts, whereof I take this that you call love to be a
            sect or scion.

RODERIGO   It cannot be.

IAGO   It is merely a lust of the blood and a permission of the will. Come,
            be a man! Drown thyself? Drown cats and blind puppies. I have   325
            professed me thy friend, and I confess me knit to thy deserving with
            cables of perdurable toughness. I could never better stead thee than
            now. Put money in thy purse. Follow thou the wars; defeat thy favour
            with an usurped beard. I say put money in thy purse. It cannot be long
            that Desdemona should continue her love to the Moor – put money in   330
            thy purse – nor he his to her; it was a violent commencement in her,
            and thou shalt see an answerable sequestration. Put but money in thy
            purse. These Moors are changeable in their wills. Fill thy purse with
            money. The food that to him now is as luscious as locusts shall be to
            him shortly as bitter as coloquintida. She must change for youth; when   335
            she is sated with his body she will find the errors of her choice.
            Therefore put money in thy purse. If thou wilt needs damn thyself, do it

338   *delicate* pleasing

339   *sanctimony* religious obedience. *erring* wandering

339–40   *super-subtle* very sophisticated

341   *enjoy* have sex with. *A pox of* forget about

342   *clean out of the way* a ridiculous idea

343   *compassing* achieving

344   *fast to* faithful to. *issue* outcome

346   *hearted* heart-felt

347   *be conjunctive* work together

348   *cuckold him* persuade his wife to be unfaithful to him

349   *Traverse* about turn (a military term – Iago means 'off you go')

353   *betimes* early

How could Iago's insincerity and manipulation of Roderigo be shown in these lines by gestures, facial expression and movements? How might Iago act differently after Roderigo has left?

356   *make my fool my purse* use this fool to provide me with money

358   *snipe* a small game bird (used here to mean a fool)

360   *thought abroad* generally believed

360–1   *'twixt … office* had sex with my wife

362–3   *for mere … surety* it is only a suspicion but I will take it as if it were true

363   *holds me well* thinks well of me

365   *proper* handsome

366   *plume up my will* do as I want

367   *double knavery* committing a double crime (i.e. getting rid of Cassio and making Othello suffer)

369   *he is too familiar* i.e. Cassio

370   *dispose* manner

371   *To be suspected* which could easily make Othello suspect him

372   *free* generous

376   *engendered* conceived

377   *monstrous* unnatural

How does Iago act in this scene compared to his actions so far in the play? Is Othello's behaviour here in keeping with what you have seen of him so far?

The Turkish fleet threatens and Othello's skills as a soldier are needed. Brabantio's complaints are heard but, when Desdemona supports Othello, that is all brushed aside and Othello is sent to Cyprus as Governor to defend the island against the Turks.

a more delicate way than drowning. Make all the money thou canst. If sanctimony and a frail vow betwixt an erring barbarian and a super-subtle Venetian be not too hard for my wits, and all the tribe of hell, 340 thou shalt enjoy her. Therefore make money. A pox of drowning thyself! It is clean out of the way. Seek thou rather to be hanged in compassing thy joy than to be drowned and go without her.

RODERIGO   Wilt thou be fast to my hopes, if I depend on the issue?

IAGO   Thou art sure of me. Go, make money. I have told thee often, and I 345 re-tell thee again and again, I hate the Moor. My cause is hearted; thine hath no less reason. Let us be conjunctive in our revenge against him. If thou canst cuckold him, thou dost thyself a pleasure, me a sport. There are many events in the womb of time, which will be delivered. Traverse, go, provide thy money. We will have more of this tomorrow. Adieu. 350

RODERIGO   Where shall we meet i' the' morning?

IAGO   At my lodging.

RODERIGO   I'll be with thee betimes.

IAGO   Go to, farewell. Do you hear, Roderigo?

RODERIGO   I'll sell all my land.   [*Exit* 355

IAGO   Thus do I ever make my fool my purse;
For I mine own gained knowledge should profane
If I would time expend with such a snipe
But for my sport and profit. I hate the Moor,
And it is thought abroad that 'twixt my sheets   360
He's done my office. I know not if 't be true,
But I, for mere suspicion in that kind,
Will do as if for surety. He holds me well;
The better shall my purpose work on him.
Cassio's a proper man; let me see now –   365
To get his place, and to plume up my will
In double knavery – how? How? Let's see.
After some time, to abuse Othello's ears
That he is too familiar with his wife.
He hath a person and a smooth dispose   370
To be suspected – framed to make women false.
The Moor is of a free and open nature
That thinks men honest that but seem to be so,
And will as tenderly be led by th' nose
As asses are.   375
I have't! It is engendered. Hell and night
Must bring this monstrous birth to the world's light.   [*Exit*

2:1

The action now moves to Cyprus. A storm is raging and news arrives that the Turkish fleet has been scattered. Cassio's ship arrives, closely followed by another carrying Iago, Desdemona and Emilia. Othello's ship arrives and he is reunited with Desdemona. Iago tells Roderigo that Desdemona is in love with Cassio. Iago begins to develop his plan of revenge.

2 *high wrought flood* very rough sea

3 *main* sea

4 *Descry* catch sight of

6 *fuller* more powerful

7 *ruffianed* blown violently

8 *ribs of oak* the wooden ribs of the ship

9 *hold the mortise* hold their joints together

10 *segregation* scattering

12 *The chidden … pelt* waves whipped up by the wind seem to beat

13 *high and monstrous main* the full power of the sea

14 *burning Bear* brightly shining constellation of the Little Bear (Ursa Minor)

15 *guards of the ever-fixèd Pole* bright stars that shine near the Pole star (The stars are used as important navigation markers.)

16 *like molestation* such a disturbance

17 *enchafèd flood* angry sea

18 *ensheltered and embayed* sheltering in a bay

19 *bear it out* survive the storm

The storm dominates the first part of the scene. If you were producing a performance of the play, how would you present this scene to create maximum dramatic effect? Where would the actors be? Would they be standing on a harbour wall? A cliff-top? A beach? Do the actors look off-stage to the right or left as if looking out to sea or would they look out over the audience as if straining to see into the distance? Would you use lighting effects to create an impression of lightning? What about the sound of wind, thunder or waves breaking? How about a fan off-stage blowing the cloaks and hair of the actors?

21 *banged* beaten

22 *designment halts* plan is stopped

23 *wrack* wreck.   *sufferance* damage

26 *Veronesa* a ship from Verona (a city in the Venetian state)

29 *in full commission* has full authority to govern

32 *sadly* seriously

36 *full* complete

38 *throw out* strain our eyes

2:1   *Enter* MONTANO *and two* GENTLEMEN

MONTANO   What from the cape can you discern at sea?

FIRST GENTLEMAN Nothing at all. It is a high-wrought flood;
      I cannot 'twixt the heaven and the main
      Descry a sail.

MONTANO   Methinks the wind hath spoke aloud at land –   5
      A fuller blast ne'er shook our battlements.
      If it hath ruffianed so upon the sea,
      What ribs of oak, when mountains melt on them,
      Can hold the mortise? What shall we hear of this?

SECOND GENTLEMAN A segregation of the Turkish fleet.   10
      For do but stand upon the foaming shore,
      The chidden billow seems to pelt the clouds;
      The wind-shaked surge, with high and monstrous main,
      Seems to cast water on the burning Bear
      And quench the guards of the ever-fixèd Pole.   15
      I never did like molestation view
      On the enchafèd flood.

MONTANO   If that the Turkish fleet
      Be not ensheltered and embayed, they are drowned:
      It is impossible to bear it out.

                Enter a third GENTLEMAN

THIRD GENTLEMAN News, lads! Our wars are done.   20
      The desperate tempest hath so banged the Turks
      That their designment halts. A noble ship of Venice
      Hath seen a grievous wrack and sufferance
      On most part of their fleet.

MONTANO   How? Is this true?

THIRD GENTLEMAN   The ship is here put in,   25
      A Veronesa. Michael Cassio,
      Lieutenant to the warlike Moor, Othello,
      Is come on shore; the Moor himself at sea,
      And is in full commission here for Cyprus.

MONTANO   I am glad on 't. 'Tis a worthy governor.   30

THIRD GENTLEMAN But this same Cassio, though he speak of comfort
      Touching the Turkish loss, yet he looks sadly
      And prays the Moor be safe; for they were parted
      With foul and violent tempest.

MONTANO   Pray heavens he be;
      For I have served him, and the man commands   35
      Like a full soldier. Let's to the sea-side, ho!
      As well to see the vessel that's come in
      As to throw out our eyes for brave Othello,

> The audience is kept informed of the developing events through the conversation of the third gentleman and Montano. The gentleman brings news of Cassio's safe arrival and the destruction of the Turks but is worried about the safety of Othello. How could his tone of voice, body movements, facial expression give a sense of these mixed emotions? What would be Montano's attitude when he says in lines 36–8:

>

Let's to the sea-side, ho!
As well to see the vessel that's come in
As to throw out our eyes for brave Othello,

39–40 *Even till … regard* until we cannot see the difference between the sea and the sky

41–2 *every minute … arrivance* we are expecting the arrival of more ships every minute

44 *approve* praise

47 *well shipped* in a good ship

48 *bark* ship

49 *Of very expert and approved allowance* experienced and with a good reputation

50 *not surfeited to death* though not over-confident

51 *Stand in bold cure* we are optimistic

53 *brow* cliff-top

55 *My hopes do shape him* I hope it is

56 *discharge their shot of courtesy* fire a salute

60 *wived* married

61 *achieved* won

62 *paragons … fame* surpasses description and wild rumour

63 *excels … pens* is even better than the ingenious descriptions of writers who praise her

64–5 *And in … ingener* her natural beauty wears out the imaginations of those who try to create a picture of her

69 *guttered* jagged
congregated sands sandbanks

70 *Traitors … keel* treacherously submerged to impede the keel of innocent ships

71 *As having* as if they have

71–2 *do omit … natures* leave aside their deadly natures

Even till we make the main and the aerial blue
An indistinct regard.

THIRD GENTLEMAN   Come, let's do so,   **40**
For every minute is expectancy
Of more arrivance.

Enter CASSIO

CASSIO   Thanks, you the valiant of the warlike isle,
That so approve the Moor! Oh, let the heavens
Give him defence against the elements,   **45**
For I have lost him on a dangerous sea.

MONTANO   Is he well shipped?

CASSIO   His bark is stoutly timbered, and his pilot
Of very expert and approved allowance;
Therefore my hopes, not surfeited to death,   **50**
Stand in bold cure.

VOICE OFF-STAGE   A sail, a sail, a sail!

CASSIO   What noise?

FIRST GENTLEMAN   The town is empty; on the brow o' the' sea
Stand ranks of people, and they cry, 'A sail!'

CASSIO   My hopes do shape him for the Governor.   **55**

Sound of cannon

SECOND GENTLEMAN   They do discharge their shot of courtesy:
Our friends at least.

CASSIO   I pray you, sir, go forth
And give us truth who 'tis that is arrived.

SECOND GENTLEMAN   I shall   [*Exit*

MONTANO   But, good Lieutenant, is your General wived?   **60**

CASSIO   Most fortunately. He hath achieved a maid
That paragons description and wild fame;
One that excels the quirks of blazoning pens,
And in the essential vesture of creation
Does tire the ingener.

Enter SECOND GENTLEMAN

                    How now? Who has put in?   **65**

SECOND GENTLEMAN   'Tis one Iago, Ancient to the General.

CASSIO   He's had most favourable and happy speed:
Tempests themselves, high seas, and howling winds,
The guttered rocks and congregated sands,
Traitors ensteeped to enclog the guiltless keel,   **70**
As having sense of beauty do omit
Their mortal natures, letting go safely by
The divine Desdemona.

75   *bold* courageous

76   *footing* landing

76–7   *anticipates … speed* comes a week earlier than we had anticipated

81   *extincted* downcast

84   *let her have your knees* kneel before her

87   *enwheel thee round* surround you

89   *aught* anything

92   *contention of sea and skies* storm

93   *Parted our fellowship* separated us

Notice how the grouping of the main characters has changed and Cassio is now at the centre of things. What tone of voice would Cassio use when he speaks of Desdemona as **our great Captain's Captain**. *Would it be sarcastic? Admiring? Amused? Would he take her hand, perhaps kiss it, bow before her, hug her?*

95   *give this greeting* fire this salute

98   *gall your patience* annoy you

99   *extend my manners* greet your wife in this way (There is a suggestion that Cassio is overdoing the normal courteous greeting.)
breeding upbringing

101–2   *would she … me* if she gave you her lips as freely as she gives me her tongue (by nagging)

103   *She has no speech* she has nothing to say

105   *still* always

106   *Marry* certainly

MONTANO	What is she?

CASSIO   She that I spake of, our great Captain's Captain,
Left in the conduct of the bold Iago,   75
Whose footing here anticipates our thoughts
A se'nnight's speed. Great Jove, Othello guard,
And swell his sail with thine own powerful breath,
That he may bless this bay with his tall ship,
Make love's quick pants in Desdemona's arms,   80
Give renewed fire to our extinguished spirits,
And bring all Cyprus comfort.

Enter DESDEMONA, IAGO, RODERIGO *and* EMILIA

    Oh, behold,
The riches of the ship is come on shore!
You men of Cyprus, let her have your knees.
Hail to thee, lady, and the grace of heaven,   85
Before, behind thee, and on every hand,
Enwheel thee round!

DESDEMONA   I thank you, valiant Cassio.
What tidings can you tell me of my lord?

CASSIO   He is not yet arrived, nor know I aught
But that he's well, and will be shortly here.   90

DESDEMONA   Oh, but I fear! How lost you company?

CASSIO   The great contention of sea and skies
Parted our fellowship.

VOICE OFF-STAGE   A sail, a sail!

CASSIO   But hark, a sail!

Sound of cannon

SECOND GENTLEMAN   They give this greeting to the citadel: 95
This likewise is a friend.

CASSIO   See for the news.

[*Exit* SECOND GENTLEMAN

Good Ancient, you are welcome. [*To* EMILIA] Welcome, mistress.
Let it not gall your patience, good Iago,
That I extend my manners; 'tis my breeding
That gives me this bold show of courtesy.   [*Kisses* EMILIA   100

IAGO   Sir, would she give you so much of her lips
As of her tongue she oft bestows on me,
You would have enough.

DESDEMONA   Alas, she has no speech.

IAGO   In faith, too much.
I find it still when I have leave to sleep.   105
Marry, before your ladyship, I grant

107–8 *puts her tongue … thinking* she keeps some things in her heart and nags in her thoughts

109 *pictures* silent

110 *Bells* noisy

111 *Saints … injuries* you put on an innocent act when attacking someone

112 *Players…housewifery* you only play at doing housewife's tasks
housewives in your beds you only take your work seriously in bed

113 *fie upon thee* shame on you

114 *Turk* a barbarian (a term of insult – Turks as non-Christians were regarded as heathens)

118 *put me to it* insist upon it

120 *assay* try

122–3 *beguile / The thing I am* I distract myself from the mood I am in (She is worried about Othello.)

125 *invention* ideas

126 *pate* head
birdlime a sticky substance used to trap birds
frieze coarse woollen cloth

127 *Muse labours* inspiration is struggling

128 *is delivered* gives birth to

129 *wit* intelligence

131 *black* dark-haired (Blondes were fashionable in Shakespeare's time.)

133 *white* a pun on the word 'wight' meaning a person or a man

136 *folly* foolishness over men (sexual connotations)
to an heir to get a rich husband

137 *fond paradoxes* foolish riddles

139 *foul* unattractive

Some critics have pointed to the problem of Desdemona seeming to engage in light-hearted banter with Iago while at the same time worrying about whether Othello is safe. How could the part of Desdemona be played in this section to make the two different moods interesting and reveal her character?

142–3 *One that … malice itself* a woman so virtuous that she gains the approval of even the most malicious

145 *Had tongue at will* spoke her mind

> She puts her tongue a little in her heart
> And chides with thinking.

EMILIA   You have little cause to say so.

IAGO   Come on, come on! You are pictures out of door;
> Bells in your parlours, wild-cats in your kitchens;   **110**
> Saints in your injuries, devils being offended;
> Players in your housewifery, and housewives in your beds.

DESDEMONA   Oh, fie upon thee, slanderer!

IAGO   Nay, it is true, or else I am a Turk –
> You rise to play, and go to bed to work.   **115**

EMILIA   You shall not write my praise.

IAGO   No, let me not.

DESDEMONA   What wouldst write of me, if thou shouldst praise me?

IAGO   Oh, gentle lady, do not put me to it,
> For I am nothing if not critical.

DESDEMONA   Come on, assay. – There's one gone to the harbour?   **120**

IAGO   Ay, madam.

DESDEMONA   I am not merry; but I do beguile
> The thing I am by seeming otherwise.
> Come, how wouldst thou praise me?

IAGO   I am about it, but indeed my invention   **125**
> Comes from my pate as birdlime does from frieze –
> It plucks out brains and all. But my Muse labours,
> And thus she is delivered:
> If she be fair and wise – fairness and wit,
> The one's for use, and the other useth it.   **130**

DESDEMONA   Well praised! How if she be black and witty?

IAGO   If she be black, and thereto have a wit,
> She'll find a white that shall her blackness fit.

DESDEMONA   Worse and worse!

EMILIA   How if fair and foolish?

IAGO   She never yet was foolish that was fair,   **135**
> For even her folly helped her to an heir.

DESDEMONA   These are old fond paradoxes to make fools laugh i' the alehouse.
> What miserable praise hast thou for her that's foul and foolish?

IAGO   There's none so foul, and foolish thereunto,
> But does foul pranks which fair and wise ones do.   **140**

DESDEMONA   Oh heavy ignorance! Thou praisest the worst best. But what praise
> couldst thou bestow on a deserving woman indeed? One that in the
> authority of her merit did justly put on the vouch of very malice itself?

IAGO   She that was ever fair, and never proud,
> Had tongue at will, and yet was never loud,   **145**

146   *gay* gaudily dressed

147   *Fled from her wish* did not do what she wanted
       yet said 'Now I may' and yet could do when appropriate

149   *Bade her … fly* refused to be angry about wrong done to her

151   *To change … tail* to exchange an ugly lover for a handsome one
       ('Cod' and 'tail' were used as terms for 'penis'.)

154   *wight* person

156   *chronicle small beer* keep track of trivial household things

157   *impotent* weak

159   *profane and liberal* irreverent and licentious

160   *home* bluntly
       relish him more in appreciate him more as

162   *well said* well done

164   *gyve* ensnare
       in thine own courtship through your own courtly behaviour

165   *tricks* behaviour

166   *kissed your three fingers* an affected courtly gesture

169   *clyster-pipes* an enema syringe

Look at Iago's description of Cassio's actions here. What is the purpose of this aside (lines 162–9)? What actions should Cassio perform here? What impressions of Cassio and Iago would you want to convey to the audience if you were directing this scene?

178   *Olympus* as high as Mount Olympus (in mythology, the home of
       the Greek gods)

179   *If it were now to die* if I were to die now

181   *content so absolute* such absolute happiness

Never lacked gold, and yet went never gay,
Fled from her wish, and yet said 'Now I may',
She that being angered, her revenge being nigh,
Bade her wrong stay, and her displeasure fly,
She that in wisdom never was so frail   150
To change the cod's head for the salmon's tail,
She that could think, and ne'er disclose her mind,
See suitors following, and not look behind:
She was a wight (if ever such wights were) –

DESDEMONA To do what?   155

IAGO   To suckle fools and chronicle small beer.

DESDEMONA Oh most lame and impotent conclusion! Do not learn of him,
Emilia, though he be thy husband. How say you, Cassio? Is he not a
most profane and liberal counsellor?

CASSIO   He speaks home, madam; you may relish him more in the soldier   160
than in the scholar.

                                        [*He takes her hand*

IAGO [*Aside*] He takes her by the palm. Ay, well said, whisper! With as little a
web as this will I ensnare as great a fly as Cassio. Ay, smile upon her,
do! I will gyve thee in thine own courtship. – You say true; 'tis so,
indeed. – If such tricks as these strip you out of your lieutenantry, it had   165
been better you had not kissed your three fingers so oft, which now
again you are most apt to play the sir in. Very good! Well kissed! An
excellent courtesy! 'Tis so indeed. Yet again your fingers to your lips?
Would they were clyster-pipes for your sake.

                            Sound of trumpet

[*Aloud*] The Moor! I know his trumpet.

CASSIO   'Tis truly so.   170

DESDEMONA Let's meet him and receive him.

CASSIO   Lo, where he comes!

                    Enter OTHELLO *and* ATTENDANTS

OTHELLO   O my fair warrior!

DESDEMONA   My dear Othello!

OTHELLO   It gives me wonder great as my content
To see you here before me. O my soul's joy!
If after every tempest come such calms,   175
May the winds blow till they have wakened death,
And let the labouring bark climb hills of seas
Olympus-high, and duck again as low
As hell's from heaven. If it were now to die,
'Twere now to be most happy; for I fear   180
My soul hath her content so absolute
That not another comfort like to this

183   *Succeeds in unknown fate* yet to come is the unknown future

187   *here* in my heart

188   *And this, and this* He kisses Desdemona.

189   *well tuned* in harmony with each other

190   *set down the pegs* loosen the tuning pegs (to create discord)

191   *As honest as I am* Iago is referring ironically to his reputation for honesty.

193   *my old acquaintance* my old friends

194   *well desired* well liked

196   *prattle out of fashion* chatter inappropriately

196–7   *dote … comforts* talk foolishly about my own happiness

198   *disembark my coffers* unload my luggage

199   *Master* ship's captain
      citadel fortress

201   *challenge* demand

203   *presently* straightaway

204   *base* dishonourable

205   *native to them* natural to them
      list listen

206   *watches* is on night watch duty
      on the court of guard at the guardhouse

207   *directly* certainly

209   *Lay thy finger thus* put your finger to your lips (i.e. keep quiet)
      Mark me note

Roderigo enters at line 82 along with Desdemona, Iago and Emilia, but he does not speak until line 208. What has he been doing on stage whilst the action has been going on? Has he been watching Desdemona? Should he move close to her? Should he watch Cassio speaking to her? Should he laugh at the banter between her and Iago? How should he react when Othello enters? What facial expressions might he show at this point?

210   *but for* merely for

211   *fantastical* fanciful
      prating empty, boastful talk
      discreet wise

213   *the devil* Othello (The devil was often depicted as black.)
      blood passions
      dull bored
      act of sport sex

214   *satiety a fresh appetite* renew her desires

215   *favour* appearance. *sympathy* similarity

217   *conveniences* desirable qualities

218   *heave the gorge* feel sick, vomit
      disrelish and abhor lose the taste for and be disgusted by
      very nature natural instincts

        Succeeds in unknown fate.

DESDEMONA   The heavens forbid
        But that our loves and comforts should increase
        Even as our days do grow.

OTHELLO   Amen to that, sweet powers!   185
        I cannot speak enough of this content;
        It stops me here: it is too much of joy.

                                        [*Kisses* **DESDEMONA**

        And this, and this, the greatest discords be
        That e'er our hearts shall make.

IAGO [*Aside*]   Oh, you are well tuned now!
        But I'll set down the pegs that make this music,   190
        As honest as I am.

OTHELLO   Come, let us to the castle.
        News, friends! Our wars are done: the Turks are drowned.
        How does my old acquaintance of this isle?
        Honey, you shall be well desired in Cyprus:
        I have found great love amongst them. Oh my sweet,   195
        I prattle out of fashion, and I dote
        In mine own comforts. I prithee, good Iago,
        Go to the bay and disembark my coffers;
        Bring thou the Master to the citadel:
        He is a good one, and his worthiness   200
        Does challenge much respect. Come, Desdemona,
        Once more well met at Cyprus!

                        [*Exeunt all but* **IAGO**, **RODERIGO** *and an* **ATTENDANT**

IAGO   Do thou meet me presently at the harbour.

                                        [*Exit* **ATTENDANT**

        Come hither. If thou be'st valiant – as they say base men being in love
        have then a nobility in their natures more than is native to them – list   205
        me. The Lieutenant tonight watches on the court of guard. First, I must
        tell thee this: Desdemona is directly in love with him.

RODERIGO   With him? Why, 'tis not possible.

IAGO   Lay thy finger thus, and let thy soul be instructed. Mark me with
        what violence she first loved the Moor but for bragging and telling her   210
        fantastical lies. To love him still for prating – let not thy discreet heart
        think it! Her eye must be fed; and what delight shall she have to look on
        the devil? When the blood is made dull with the act of sport, there
        should be, again to inflame it and to give satiety a fresh appetite,
        loveliness in favour, sympathy in years, manners and beauties – all   215
        which the Moor is defective in. Now for want of these required
        conveniences, her delicate tenderness will find itself abused, begin to
        heave the gorge, disrelish and abhor the Moor; very nature will instruct
        her in it and compel her to some second choice. Now, sir, this granted –

220   *pregnant and unforced position*   plausible and natural position

221   *the degree of this fortune*   stands most to benefit from this
         A knave very voluble   a smooth-talking scoundrel

221–2   *no further conscionable*   with no more conscience

223   *seeming*   outward appearance
         compass   achieving.
         salt   lustful

224   *loose affection*   immoral desires
         slipper and subtle   slippery and cunning

225   *finder of occasion*   opportunist

225–6   *can stamp … advantages*   can create opportunities that are to his advantage

228   *requisites*   desirable qualities
         folly and green minds look after   wanton and naïve women look for

Iago works on Roderigo

231   *The wine … grapes*   she is like all women

239   *mutualities*   shared intimacies
         marshal the way   lead the way
         hard at hand   close at hand

239–40   *master and main exercise*   the main action

240   *the incorporate conclusion*   the physical result (i.e. sex)

244   *tainting his discipline*   mocking his ability as a soldier

246   *Well*   agreed

247   *sudden in choler*   quick to anger
         haply   perhaps

249   *to mutiny*   to lose confidence

249–50   *whose qualification … of Cassio*   who will not be satisfied until Cassio has been dismissed

251   *prefer*   promote

252   *the impediment*   i.e. Cassio

253   *prosperity*   success

255–6   *his necessaries*   Othello's belongings

259   *apt and of great credit*   likely and very believable

260   *howbeit that*   although

261   *constant*   faithful

as it is a most pregnant and unforced position – who stands so eminent   220
in the degree of this fortune as Cassio does? – A knave very voluble, no
further conscionable than in putting on the mere form of civil and
humane seeming for the better compass of his salt and most hidden
loose affection. – Why, none! Why, none! A slipper and subtle knave, a
finder of occasion, that has an eye can stamp and counterfeit   225
advantages, though true advantage never present itself; a devilish
knave! Besides, the knave is handsome, young, and has all those
requisites in him that folly and green minds look after. A pestilent
complete knave, and the woman hath found him already.

RODERIGO   I cannot believe that in her – she's full of most blessed condition.   230

IAGO   Blessed fig's end! The wine she drinks is made of grapes. If she had
been blessed, she would never have loved the Moor. Blessed pudding!
Didst thou not see her paddle with the palm of his hand? Didst not
mark that?

RODERIGO   Yes, that I did: but that was but courtesy.   235

IAGO   Lechery, by this hand! An index and obscure prologue to the
history of lust and foul thoughts! They met so near with their lips that
their breaths embraced together. Villainous thoughts, Roderigo! When
these mutualities so marshal the way, hard at hand comes the master
and main exercise, the incorporate conclusion. Pish! But, sir, be you   240
ruled by me. I have brought you from Venice. Watch you tonight; for
the command, I'll lay it upon you. Cassio knows you not. I'll not be far
from you. Do you find some occasion to anger Cassio, either by
speaking too loud or tainting his discipline, or from what other course
you please which the time shall more favourably minister.   245

RODERIGO   Well.

IAGO   Sir, he's rash and very sudden in choler, and haply may strike at
you. Provoke him that he may; for even out of that will I cause these of
Cyprus to mutiny, whose qualification shall come into no true taste
again but by the displanting of Cassio. So shall you have a shorter   250
journey to your desires by the means I shall then have to prefer them;
and the impediment most profitably removed without the which there
were no expectation of our prosperity.

RODERIGO   I will do this, if you can bring it to any opportunity.

IAGO   I warrant thee. Meet me by and by at the citadel. I must fetch his   255
necessaries ashore. Farewell.

RODERIGO   Adieu.   [*Exit*

IAGO   That Cassio loves her, I do well believe it;
That she loves him, 'tis apt and of great credit.
The Moor – howbeit that I endure him not –   260
Is of a constant, loving, noble nature,
And I dare think he'll prove to Desdemona
A most dear husband. Now, I do love her too;

264 *Not ... lust* not only out of lust. *peradventure* perhaps

265 *stand accountant* responsible

266 *diet* feed

267 *For that* because

268 *leaped into my seat* had sex with my wife

269 *mineral* drug. *inwards* insides

275 *poor trash of Venice* i.e. Roderigo. *trace* pursue

276 *stand the putting on* is up to being incited

277 *on the hip* at my mercy

278 *Abuse* slander. *right garb* using appropriate language

279 *with my night-cap* I think that Cassio has slept with my wife too

281 *egregiously* flagrantly

282 *practising upon* plotting against

283 *'Tis here* i.e. in my head

> Look at Iago's soliloquy at the end of the scene. Compare the motives that he gives here for plotting his revenge with those he gives in his first soliloquy in Act 1 Scene 2. Are they the same? Are they different? What do you think that Shakespeare is showing his audience about Iago?

Othello has arrived safely and is reunited with Desdemona. Iago's plot begins to take shape as he decides to make Othello suspicious that Desdemona is having an affair with Cassio and therefore sow the seeds of jealousy in his mind.

2:2

A herald announces that the Turkish fleet has been destroyed. Othello wants everyone to celebrate both the defeat of the enemy and his marriage to Desdemona.

1 *pleasure* wish

2 *certain tidings* definite news. *importing* giving new of. *mere perdition* total destruction

3 *triumph* victory celebrations

4 *addition* social position

5 *beneficial* good. *nuptial* marriage

6 *offices* stores for food and drink

8 *told* struck

> *Would you have a small crowd gathered or just two or three actors? Would Iago, Cassio and the others be there? Would they go wild at the news, congratulate each other, cheer, shout, throw their hats in the air? What would you have done?*

> Compare the mood created here with that at the beginning of Scene 1. Is it the same? Is it different? If so, how? What kind of atmosphere does Shakespeare create here? Relieved? Joyful? Subdued?

The threat of invasion has passed and Othello wants to enjoy the celebration of his wedding night.

Not out of absolute lust – though peradventure
I stand accountant for as great a sin – 265
But partly led to diet my revenge
For that I do suspect the lusty Moor
Hath leaped into my seat; the thought whereof
Doth like a poisonous mineral gnaw my inwards;
And nothing can, or shall, content my soul 270
Till I am evened with him, wife for wife;
Or failing so, yet that I put the Moor
At least into a jealousy so strong
That judgment cannot cure. Which thing to do,
If this poor trash of Venice, whom I trace 275
For his quick hunting, stand the putting on,
I'll have our Michael Cassio on the hip,
Abuse him to the Moor in the right garb
(For I fear Cassio with my night-cap too),
Make the Moor thank me, love me, and reward me, 280
For making him egregiously an ass
And practising upon his peace and quiet
Even to madness. 'Tis here, but yet confused:
Knavery's plain face is never seen till used.

[*Exit*

2:2   *Enter* HERALD *with a proclamation*

HERALD   It is Othello's pleasure, our noble and valiant General, that upon
certain tidings now arrived, importing the mere perdition of the Turkish
fleet, every man put himself into triumph: some to dance, some to make
bonfires, each man to what sport and revels his addition leads him. For,
besides these beneficial news, it is the celebration of his nuptial. So 5
much was his pleasure should be proclaimed. All offices are open, and
there is full liberty of feasting from this present hour of five till the bell
have told eleven. Bless the isle of Cyprus, and our noble General
Othello.

[*Exit*

2:3

Othello places Cassio in charge of making sure that the celebrations do not get out of hand. Iago gets Cassio drunk. Cassio beats Roderigo and a fight breaks out in which Cassio wounds Montano. Othello is disturbed and dismisses Cassio as his lieutenant. Iago persuades Cassio to ask Desdemona to plead on his behalf with Othello. Iago also hints that Desdemona is concerned about Cassio because she is in love with him.

1	*look you to*	you take charge
2	*stop*	restraint
3	*Not to outsport discretion*	not to let the celebrations get out of hand
4	*hath direction*	has been instructed
5	*notwithstanding*	nevertheless
6	*honest*	reliable, dependable (another of the many references to Iago as 'honest')
7	*with your earliest*	as early as possible
9	*The purchase made*	the problems relating to our marriage are over
	the fruits are to ensue	the enjoyment is yet to come
10	*profit*	pleasure
13	*Not this hour*	not yet
14	*cast*	dismissed
15	*made wanton the night*	had a night of love-making
18	*full of game*	always ready for sex
20	*sounds a parley to provocation*	provokes sexual interest
21	*inviting*	attractive
	methinks right modest	I think she is completely innocent
22	*alarum*	a call to action
24	*stoup*	large tankard
25	*brace*	pair
	Cyprus gallants	gentlemen from Cyprus
	would fain	are keen to
26	*have a measure*	drink a toast
27–8	*I have … for drinking*	I get drunk very easily
28	*courtesy*	social convention
31	*craftily qualified*	cleverly mixed with water
32	*innovation*	change
33	*infirmity*	weakness

2:3   *Enter* OTHELLO, DESDEMONA, CASSIO *and* ATTENDANTS

OTHELLO   Good Michael, look you to the guard tonight.
  Let's teach ourselves that honourable stop,
  Not to outsport discretion.

CASSIO   Iago hath direction what to do;
  But notwithstanding, with my personal eye   5
  Will I look to it.

OTHELLO   Iago is most honest.
  Michael, good night. Tomorrow with your earliest
  Let me have speech with you. [*To* DESDEMONA] Come, my dear love,
  The purchase made, the fruits are to ensue;
  That profit's yet to come 'tween me and you.   10
  Good night.

  [*Exeunt* OTHELLO, DESDEMONA *and* ATTENDANTS

  Enter IAGO

CASSIO   Welcome, Iago. We must to the watch.

IAGO   Not this hour, Lieutenant; 'tis not yet ten o' th' clock. Our General
  cast us thus early for the love of his Desdemona; who let us not
  therefore blame – he hath not yet made wanton the night with her, and   15
  she is sport for Jove.

CASSIO   She's a most exquisite lady.

IAGO   And, I'll warrant her, full of game.

CASSIO   Indeed, she's a most fresh and delicate creature.

IAGO   What an eye she has! Methinks it sounds a parley to provocation.   20

CASSIO   An inviting eye, and yet methinks right modest.

IAGO   And when she speaks, is it not an alarum to love?

CASSIO   She is indeed perfection.

IAGO   Well, happiness to their sheets! Come, Lieutenant, I have a stoup of
  wine, and here without are a brace of Cyprus gallants that would fain   25
  have a measure to the health of black Othello.

CASSIO   Not tonight, good Iago. I have very poor and unhappy brains for
  drinking. I could well wish courtesy would invent some other custom of
  entertainment.

IAGO   Oh, they are our friends. But one cup! I'll drink for you.   30

CASSIO   I have drunk but one cup tonight, and that was craftily qualified
  too; and behold what innovation it makes here. I am unfortunate in the
  infirmity, and dare not task my weakness with any more.

IAGO   What, man? 'Tis a night of revels; the gallants desire it.

CASSIO   Where are they?   35

37 *dislikes me* I don't like it

38 *fasten but one cup upon him* persuade him to take one more drink

40 *offence* readiness to take offence

41 *my young mistress' dog* a spoilt pet dog
sick love-sick

43 *caroused* drunk toasts

44 *Potations pottle-deep* tankards full of drink
he's to watch he's to be on guard

45 *Three else* three others
swelling arrogant

46 *That hold … wary distance* easily provoked if they feel their honour has been insulted

47 *The very elements of* typical of the kind of men

48 *flustered* befuddled

50 *put our Cassio in some action* provoke Cassio to start a quarrel

One of the advantages that Iago has is that he is able to spot people's weaknesses and exploit them to his own advantage. Here he knows exactly how to use Cassio's weakness for drink. What persuasive techniques does he use to persuade Cassio to drink? Does he put his arm around him like a friend? His tone of voice could be cajoling, or pleading. He might make Cassio feel that he owes it to him as a friend to have a drink with him. He might smile or look disappointed when Cassio won't drink with him.

52 *consequence* the result
approve my dream turns out as I hope

53 *both with wind and stream* helped by wind and current

54 *rouse* large drink

57 *canakin* small tankard

60 *span* a short time

64–5 *potent in potting* good at drinking

65 *swag-bellied Hollander* a Dutchman with a large sagging belly

67 *exquisite* expert

68 *facility* with ease

68–9 *He sweats not … Almain* he has no difficulty in overcoming a German

72 *do you justice* match you in drinking

76 *a crown* a coin

78 *lown* a cheat

IAGO	Here at the door; I pray you call them in.	
CASSIO	I'll do it, but it dislikes me.	[*Exit*
IAGO	If I can fasten but one cup upon him,	

IAGO   If I can fasten but one cup upon him,
With that which he hath drunk tonight already,
He'll be as full of quarrel and offence   40
As my young mistress' dog. Now my sick fool Roderigo,
Whom love hath turned almost the wrong side out,
To Desdemona hath tonight caroused
Potations pottle-deep; and he's to watch.
Three else of Cyprus, noble swelling spirits,   45
That hold their honours in a wary distance,
The very elements of this warlike isle,
Have I tonight flustered with flowing cups,
And they watch too. Now 'mongst this flock of drunkards
Am I to put our Cassio in some action   50
That may offend the isle. But here they come.

       Enter CASSIO, MONTANO, *two* GENTLEMEN, *and* SERVANTS *with wine*

If consequence do but approve my dream,
My boat sails freely, both with wind and stream.

CASSIO   'Fore God, they have given me a rouse already.

MONTANO   Good faith, a little one – not past a pint, as I am a soldier.   55

IAGO   Some wine, ho!
     [*Sings*]   And let me the canakin clink, clink;
           And let me the canakin clink;
             A soldier's a man,
           Oh, man's life's but a span;   60
           Why then, let a soldier drink.
       Some wine, boys!

CASSIO   'Fore God, an excellent song!

IAGO   I learned it in England, where indeed they are most potent in
potting. Your Dane, your German, and your swag-bellied Hollander –   65
drink, ho! – are nothing to your English.

CASSIO   Is your Englishman so exquisite in his drinking?

IAGO   Why, he drinks you with facility your Dane dead drunk; he sweats
not to overthrow your Almain; he gives your Hollander a vomit ere the
next pottle can be filled.   70

CASSIO   To the health of our General!

MONTANO   I am for it, Lieutenant, and I'll do you justice.

IAGO   Oh sweet England!
     [*Sings*]   King Stephen was and a worthy peer;
           His breeches cost him but a crown;   75
       He held them sixpence all too dear,
           With that he called the tailor lown.

79   *wight* man

80   *low degree* lowly birth

82   *auld* old

84   *exquisite* beautiful

86   *place* position

91   *quality* superior status

101   *platform* gun batteries
      set the watch mount guard

104   *direction* orders

105   *just equinox* exact equivalent of dark and light

106   *The one as long as the other* i.e. Cassio has vices and virtues in equal measure.

108   *odd time* chance moment
      infirmity addiction to drink

110   *evermore the prologue to his sleep* i.e. He drinks regularly before sleeping.

111   *watch the horologe a double set* he'll stay awake twice round the clock (i.e. 24 hours)

He was a wight of high renown,
    And thou art but of low degree;   **80**
'Tis pride that pulls the country down;
    And take thine auld cloak about thee.
  Some wine, ho!

CASSIO   'Fore God, this is a more exquisite song than the other.

IAGO   Will you hear 't again?   **85**

CASSIO   No, for I hold him to be unworthy of his place that does those things. Well, God's above all; and there be souls must be saved, and there be souls must not be saved.

IAGO   It's true, good Lieutenant.

CASSIO   For mine own part – no offence to the General, nor any man of   **90** quality – I hope to be saved.

IAGO   And so do I too, Lieutenant.

CASSIO   Ay, but, by your leave, not before me. The Lieutenant is to be saved before the Ancient. Let's have no more of this; let's to our affairs. God forgive us our sins. Gentlemen, let's look to our business. Do not think,   **95** gentlemen, I am drunk: this is my Ancient, this is my right hand, and this is my left. I am not drunk now: I can stand well enough, and I speak well enough.

GENTLEMEN   Excellent well!

CASSIO   Why, very well then! You must not think, then, that I am drunk.   **100**

                                          [Exit

MONTANO   To the platform, masters; come, let's set the watch.

IAGO   You see this fellow that is gone before?
He is a soldier, fit to stand by Caesar
And give direction. And do but see his vice:
'Tis to his virtue a just equinox,   **105**
The one as long as the other. 'Tis pity of him.
I fear the trust Othello puts him in,
On some odd time of his infirmity,
Will shake this island.

MONTANO   But is he often thus?

IAGO   'Tis evermore the prologue to his sleep: **110**
He'll watch the horologe a double set
If drink rock not his cradle.

MONTANO   It were well
The General were put in mind of it.
Perhaps he sees it not, or his good nature
Prizes the virtue that appears in Cassio   **115**
And looks not on his evils. Is not this true?

Enter RODERIGO

120 *hazard ... own second* take a risk with the position of his deputy

121 *ingraft* deep rooted

> If this scene is to work, it is important that the actor playing Cassio convinces the audience of his increasing drunkenness. How could an actor use the language here to create a convincing sense of Cassio's drunkenness? Does he slur his speech? Move erractically? Do his eyes look glazed? Does he show flashes of aggression? Where in the speech could you direct the actor to show any of these?

128–9 *twiggen bottle* a bottle covered with wickerwork
(i.e. beat him until he is covered with a latticework of cuts)

Hold, ho! Lieutenant! – Sir! Montano! – Gentlemen!

131 *prate* talk rubbish

133 *mazzard* cheat

136 *cry a mutiny* raise the alarm, there is a brawl

140 *Diablo, ho* what the devil

141 *rise* be awakened

142 *ashamed* dishonoured

143 *He dies* I'll kill him

IAGO [*Aside*] How now, Roderigo!
　　　　I pray you, after the Lieutenant, go!

　　　　　　　　　　　　　　　　　　[*Exit* RODERIGO

MONTANO   And 'tis great pity that the noble Moor
　　　　Should hazard such a place as his own second　　　　　　120
　　　　With one of an ingraft infirmity.
　　　　It were an honest action to say so
　　　　To the Moor.

IAGO　　　　　　　　Not I, for this fair island!
　　　　I do love Cassio well, and would do much
　　　　To cure him of this evil.

　　　　　　　　　　A cry off-stage

　　　　　　　　　　But hark, what noise?　　　　　　　　125

　　　　　　Enter CASSIO *pursuing* RODERIGO

CASSIO　　Zounds, you rogue! You rascal!

MONTANO　What's the matter, Lieutenant?

CASSIO　　A knave teach me my duty? I'll beat the knave into a twiggen
　　　　bottle!

RODERIGO　Beat me?　　　　　　　　　　　　　　　　130

CASSIO　　Dost thou prate, rogue?

MONTANO　Nay, good Lieutenant – I pray you, sir, hold your hand.

CASSIO　　Let me go, sir, or I'll knock you o'er the mazzard.

MONTANO　Come, come, you're drunk.

CASSIO　　Drunk?　　　　　　　　　　　　　　　　135

　　　　　　CASSIO *and* MONTANO *fight*

IAGO [*Aside to* RODERIGO] Away, I say: go out and cry a mutiny.　[*Exit* RODERIGO
　　　　[*Aloud*] Nay, good Lieutenant. – God's will, gentlemen! –
　　　　Help, ho! – Lieutenant! – Sir! Montano! –
　　　　Help, masters! – Here's a goodly watch indeed!

　　　　　　　　　　A bell rings

　　　　Who's that which rings the bell? Diablo, ho!　　　　140
　　　　The town will rise. – God's will, Lieutenant,
　　　　You'll be ashamed for ever.

　　　　　　Enter OTHELLO *and* ATTENDANTS

OTHELLO　　　　　　　　What is the matter here?

MONTANO　Zounds, I bleed still – I am hurt to the death. He dies!

　　　　　　　　　　　　　　　　　[*Assails* CASSIO

OTHELLO　　　Hold, for your lives!

149   *turned Turks* become as savage as the Turks

149–50   *that / Which … Ottomites* i.e. kill one another

152   *to carve for his own rage* attack to vent his own anger

153   *Holds his soul light* does not value his own life
upon his motion the instant he moves

154   *dreadful* frightening

155   *propriety* proper order

157   *love* friendship

159   *In quarter* correct in conduct

160   *Devesting* undressing

161   *As if some planet had unwitted men* as if they had gone mad (It was believed that planets coming too close to the earth could cause madness.)

162   *tilting* thrusting their swords at

164   *peevish odds* bad-tempered argument

167   *you are thus forgot* you have forgotten your position

170   *gravity and stillness* seriousness and sobriety

172   *censure* judgement

173   *unlace* undo

174   *spend* exchanging
your rich opinion the good opinions that people have of you

178   *offends me* hurts me

181   *self-charity* looking after yourself

184   *blood* anger

185   *collied* darkened

186   *Assays* tries

188   *sink in my rebuke* suffer my disciplinary action

IAGO	Hold, ho! Lieutenant! – Sir! Montano! – Gentlemen!	**145**
	Have you forgot all sense of place and duty?	
	Hold! The General speaks to you. Hold, for shame!	
OTHELLO	Why, how now, ho! From whence ariseth this?	
	Are we turned Turks, and to ourselves do that	
	Which heaven hath forbid the Ottomites?	**150**
	For Christian shame, put by this barbarous brawl!	
	He that stirs next to carve for his own rage	
	Holds his soul light – he dies upon his motion.	
	Silence that dreadful bell: it frights the isle	
	From her propriety. What is the matter, masters?	**155**
	Honest Iago, that looks dead with grieving,	
	Speak. Who began this? On thy love, I charge thee.	
IAGO	I do not know. Friends all, but now, even now;	
	In quarter and in terms like bride and groom	
	Devesting them for bed; and then, but now –	**160**
	As if some planet had unwitted men –	
	Swords out, and tilting one at other's breasts	
	In opposition bloody. I cannot speak	
	Any beginning to this peevish odds,	
	And would in action glorious I had lost	**165**
	Those legs that brought me to a part of it!	
OTHELLO	How comes it, Michael, you are thus forgot?	
CASSIO	I pray you pardon me; I cannot speak.	
OTHELLO	Worthy Montano, you were wont to be civil;	
	The gravity and stillness of your youth	**170**
	The world hath noted, and your name is great	
	In mouths of wisest censure. What's the matter	
	That you unlace your reputation thus,	
	And spend your rich opinion for the name	
	Of a night-brawler? Give me answer to it.	**175**
MONTANO	Worthy Othello, I am hurt to danger.	
	Your officer, Iago, can inform you –	
	While I spare speech, which something now offends me –	
	Of all that I do know; nor know I aught	
	By me that's said or done amiss this night,	**180**
	Unless self-charity be sometimes a vice,	
	And to defend ourselves it be a sin	
	When violence assails us.	
OTHELLO	Now by heaven,	
	My blood begins my safer guides to rule,	
	And passion, having my best judgment collied,	**185**
	Assays to lead the way. Zounds, if I stir	
	Or do but lift this arm, the best of you	
	Shall sink in my rebuke. Give me to know	

189   *rout* brawl

190   *approved in* proved guilty

192   *lose me* lose my trust and friendship

193   *Yet wild* still volatile

194   *manage* carry out

195   *on the court and guard of safety* on duty at the guardroom

> *Othello's language here shows giveaway signs of his temper beginning to rise. What particular words or phrases express this feeling? How might Othello speak them? Overall, though, he still keeps his control in a dignified and commanding way. What is the dominant impression of him at this point in the play?*

197   *partially affined* influenced by friendship
      leagued in office in league with Cassio as a brother officer

198   *deliver* testify

199   *Touch me not so near* don't remind me of things that are so important to me

207   *to execute upon him* attach him
      this gentleman i.e. Montano

208   *steps in to* blocks Cassio's way
      entreats his pause pleads with him to stop

212   *rather* all the more quickly

213   *For that* because

214   *high in oath* swearing loudly

220   *forget* forget themselves

224   *strange indignity* unknown insult

225   *patience could not pass* even the most patient person could not tolerate

226   *mince this matter* play down the seriousness of this

> *Iago's skill lies in using words to suggest a certain idea without actually saying it. He uses this skill to manipulate Othello's response. Look at Iago's speech, lines 199–225. Which phrases suggest that he is covering up for Cassio by making light of the incident? What tone might Iago use to speak these lines? Does he sound dismissive of the trouble? Reluctant to speak? Evasive?*

How this foul rout began, who set it on;
And he that is approved in this offence,   **190**
Though he had twinned with me, both at a birth,
Shall lose me. What! In a town of war,
Yet wild, the people's hearts brim-full of fear,
To manage private and domestic quarrel?
In night, and on the court and guard of safety?   **195**
'Tis monstrous! Iago, who began 't?

MONTANO   If partially affined, or leagued in office,
Thou dost deliver more, or less, than truth,
Thou art no soldier.

IAGO   Touch me not so near.
I had rather have this tongue cut from my mouth   **200**
Than it should do offence to Michael Cassio.
Yet, I persuade myself, to speak the truth
Shall nothing wrong him. This it is, General:
Montano and myself being in speech,
There comes a fellow crying out for help,   **205**
And Cassio following him with determined sword
To execute upon him. Sir, this gentleman
Steps in to Cassio and entreats his pause;
Myself the crying fellow did pursue
Lest by his clamour – as it so fell out –   **210**
The town might fall in fright. He, swift of foot,
Outran my purpose; and I returned then, rather
For that I heard the clink and fall of swords,
And Cassio high in oath – which till tonight
I ne'er might say before. When I came back –   **215**
For this was brief – I found them close together
At blow and thrust, even as again they were
When you yourself did part them.
More of this matter cannot I report.
But men are men – and best sometimes forget;   **220**
Though Cassio did some little wrong to him,
As men in rage strike those that wish them best,
Yet surely Cassio, I believe, received
From him that fled some strange indignity
Which patience could not pass.

OTHELLO   I know, Iago,   **225**
Thy honesty and love doth mince this matter,
Making it light to Cassio. Cassio, I love thee,
But never more be officer of mine.

Enter DESDEMONA *and* ATTENDANTS

Look, if my gentle love be not raised up!
I'll make thee an example.

235   *distracted* disturbed

237   *balmy* sweet

245   *sense* feeling

246   *idle* trivial
        imposition obligation

248   *recover* regain the trust of

249   *cast in his mood* temporarily dismisses because he is angry

250   *in policy* for political reasons (i.e. He had to make an example of
        Cassio because of his behaviour.)

251   *Sue* appeal

252   *deceive* betray

254   *speak parrot* speak nonsense

255   *discourse fustian* discuss things like a fool

264   *pleasance* pleasure
        applause self-approval

267   *wrath* anger
        unperfectness imperfection

269   *moraller* moraliser (i.e. He judges himself too harshly.)

Othello (Ray Fearon) is disturbed. From the 1990 RSC production

82

DESDEMONA	What is the matter, dear?	**230**

OTHELLO   All's well, sweeting; come away to bed.
[*To* **MONTANO**] Sir, for your hurts myself will be your surgeon.
Lead him off.

*[***MONTANO*** is helped off*

Iago, look with care about the town
And silence those whom this vile brawl distracted.   **235**
Come, Desdemona; 'tis the soldiers' life
To have their balmy slumbers waked with strife.

[Exeunt all but **IAGO** *and* **CASSIO**

IAGO   What, are you hurt, Lieutenant?

CASSIO   Ay, past all surgery.

IAGO   Marry, God forbid!   **240**

CASSIO   Reputation, reputation, reputation! Oh, I have lost my reputation!
I have lost the immortal part of myself, and what remains is bestial. My
reputation, Iago, my reputation!

IAGO   As I am an honest man, I had thought you had received some bodily
wound – there is more sense in that than in reputation. Reputation is   **245**
an idle and most false imposition, oft got without merit, and lost
without deserving. You have lost no reputation at all, unless you repute
yourself such a loser. What, man! There are more ways to recover the
General again. You are but now cast in his mood – a punishment more
in policy than in malice – even so as one would beat his offenceless dog   **250**
to affright an imperious lion. Sue to him again, and he's yours.

CASSIO   I will rather sue to be despised than to deceive so good a
commander with so slight, so drunken and so indiscreet an officer.
Drunk! And speak parrot! And squabble! Swagger! Swear! And
discourse fustian with one's own shadow! Oh, thou invisible spirit of   **255**
wine, if thou hast no name to be known by, let us call thee devil!

IAGO   What was he that you followed with your sword? What had he
done to you?

CASSIO   I know not.

IAGO   Is 't possible?   **260**

CASSIO   I remember a mass of things, but nothing distinctly – a quarrel, but
nothing wherefore. Oh God, that men should put an enemy in their
mouths to steal away their brains! That we should with joy, pleasance,
revel and applause transform ourselves into beasts!

IAGO   Why, but you are now well enough. How came you thus recovered?   **265**

CASSIO   It hath pleased the devil drunkenness to give place to the devil
wrath: one unperfectness shows me another, to make me frankly
despise myself.

IAGO   Come, you are too severe a moraller. As the time, the place, and the
condition of this country stands, I could heartily wish this had not   **270**

273	*Hydra* a creature from Greek mythology – a many-headed snake killed by Hercules
275	*inordinate* excessive
276	*familiar* friendly (Familiars were also evil spirits in the shape of animals that were kept by witches.)
279	*approved it* confirmed
280	*at a time* once in a while
283	*denotement of her parts* observation of her good qualities
284	*importune* beg for
285	*free* generous. *apt* willing
286	*vice* fault
287	*splinter* help to heal
285	*lay* bet
291	*protest* insist
292	*think it freely* believe it absolutely. *betimes* early
293	*undertake* take up the matter

Once again Iago's powers of manipulation are seen. What state of mind is Cassio in here and how is Iago able to take advantage of this? Look at Iago's speech, lines 280–9. Does he use a gentle, comforting tone towards Cassio? Is his advice offered in a bluff, no-nonsense, common sense manner? Does Cassio sit with his head in his hands or pace the stage full of self-anger?

293–4	*desperate of … check me here* I am desperate if this doesn't work
297	*what's he then that says* how could anyone say that
298	*free* open
299	*Probal* reasonable
301	*inclining* sympathetic *subdue* win over
302	*suit* appeal *framed as fruitful* naturally generous
303	*elements* nature
304	*were't* even if it were
305	*seals and symbols* all the signs of religion
306	*enfettered* bound
307	*list* wants
308	*her appetite* her desires
309	*weak* i.e. unable to resist *function* natural impulses
310	*counsel* advise *parallel course* in line with his interests
311	*Divinity of Hell* the Devil
312	*put on* encourage
313	*suggest* tempt *heavenly shows* the appearance of being good

befallen; but since it is as it is, mend it for your own good.

CASSIO   I will ask him for my place again; he shall tell me I am a drunkard!
Had I as many mouths as Hydra, such an answer would stop them all.
To be now a sensible man, by and by a fool, and presently a beast! Oh
strange! Every inordinate cup is unblessed and the ingredient is a devil.   275

IAGO   Come, come, good wine is a good familiar creature if it be well
used. Exclaim no more against it. And, good Lieutenant, I think you
think I love you.

CASSIO   I have well approved it, sir. I, drunk!

IAGO   You or any man living may be drunk at a time, man. I tell you what   280
you shall do. Our General's wife is now the General. I may say so in this
respect, for that he hath devoted and given up himself to the
contemplation, mark and denotement of her parts and graces. Confess
yourself freely to her; importune her help to put you in your place
again. She is of so free, so kind, so apt, so blessed a disposition, she   285
holds it a vice in her goodness not to do more than she is requested.
This broken joint between you and her husband, entreat her to splinter;
and my fortunes against any lay worth naming, this crack of your love
shall grow stronger than it was before.

CASSIO   You advise me well.   290

IAGO   I protest, in the sincerity of love and honest kindness.

CASSIO   I think it freely; and betimes in the morning I will beseech the
virtuous Desdemona to undertake for me. I am desperate of my
fortunes, if they check me here.

IAGO   You are in the right. Good night, Lieutenant; I must to the watch.   295

CASSIO   Good night, honest Iago.

[*Exit* CASSIO

IAGO   And what's he then that says I play the villain,
When this advice is free I give, and honest,
Probal to thinking, and indeed the course
To win the Moor again? For 'tis most easy   300
The inclining Desdemona to subdue
In any honest suit. She's framed as fruitful
As the free elements. And then for her
To win the Moor – were 't to renounce his baptism,
All seals and symbols of redeemèd sin,   305
His soul is so enfettered to her love
That she may make, unmake, do what she list,
Even as her appetite shall play the god,
With his weak function. How am I then a villain
To counsel Cassio to this parallel course   310
Directly to his good? Divinity of hell!
When devils will the blackest sins put on,
They do suggest at first with heavenly shows,

315	*Plies* appeals to her
317	*pestilence* poison
318	*repeals him* asks for him to be reinstated
319–20	*by how … the Moor* the more she pleads on his behalf the less Othello will trust her
325	*fills up the cry* makes up the numbers
326	*cudgelled* beaten
	issue result
332	*dilatory* slow-moving
334	*cashiered* dismissed
339	*billeted* lodged
342	*move for* speak in favour of
345	*jump* at the right moment
346	*Soliciting* pleading favours from
347	*device* plan
	coldness lack of enthusiasm

Compare Iago's words and actions towards Cassio before and after the fight. Are there any differences? Does he speak to him in the same kind of way? If his manner changes, why might this be?

Compare Othello's words and actions in this scene with his other appearances so far in the play.

Cassio is sacked as Othello's lieutenant after a drunken brawl. Iago persuades Cassio to ask Desdemona to plead his case with Othello. Iago, though, intends to make Othello believe that Desdemona is having an affair with Cassio.

As I do now. For whiles this honest fool
Plies Desdemona to repair his fortune,   315
And she for him pleads strongly to the Moor,
I'll pour this pestilence into his ear –
That she repeals him for her body's lust;
And by how much she strives to do him good
She shall undo her credit with the Moor.   320
So will I turn her virtue into pitch,
And out of her own goodness make the net
That shall enmesh them all.

Enter RODERIGO

How now, Roderigo?

RODERIGO   I do follow here in the chase, not like a hound that hunts, but one
that fills up the cry. My money is almost spent; I have been tonight   325
exceedingly well cudgelled; and I think the issue will be, I shall have so
much experience for my pains. And so, with no money at all, and a little
more wit, return again to Venice.

IAGO   How poor are they that have not patience!
What wound did ever heal but by degrees?   330
Thou know'st we work by wit, and not by witchcraft,
And wit depends on dilatory time.
Does 't not go well? Cassio hath beaten thee,
And thou by that small hurt has cashiered Cassio.
Though other things grow fair against the sun,   335
Yet fruits that blossom first will first be ripe.
Content thyself awhile. By the mass, 'tis morning!
Pleasure, and action, make the hours seem short.
Retire thee, go where thou art billeted.
Away, I say! Thou shalt know more hereafter.   340
Nay, get thee gone.   [*Exit* RODERIGO
                    Two things are to be done:
My wife must move for Cassio to her mistress;
I'll set her on –
Myself the while to draw the Moor apart
And bring him jump when he may Cassio find   345
Soliciting his wife. Ay, that's the way!
Dull not device by coldness and delay.

[*Exit*

3:1

The following morning Cassio brings musicians to wake Othello and Desdemona. The Clown is sent out to tell them to go away. Iago enters and Cassio tells him that he has asked Emilia to present his plea to Desdemona. Iago says he will send Emilia to see him and help by getting Othello out of the way. Emilia enters bringing the hopeful news that Desdemona is already pleading for Cassio. Cassio asks her to arrange for him to meet Desdemona.

1   *content your pains*   pay for your trouble

3   *Clown*   The term 'clown' has a double meaning:
(a) fool or jester who makes witty remarks;
(b) a low-life comic character. Here the Clown is a servant of Othello's household.

4   *speak i' the nose*   produce a nasal sound

7   *marry*   indeed

8   *thereby hangs a tale*   there's a story about that (There is a pun here on the word 'tale' as 'tail' was a common term for penis.)

10   *wind instrument*   another pun here, this time to do with breaking wind

14   *to 't again*   set to it again (i.e. play some more)

21   *keep up thy quillets*   stop your quibbling

23   *entreats*   begs

25–6   *seem to notify unto her*   tell her (mocking Cassio's elaborate way of speaking)

The opening part of this scene, with its music, provides a brief interlude to the fast-moving events and tense atmosphere created in the first two acts. In many performances, though, this section involving the Clown, and often the part involving the musicians too, is left out. If you were producing the play, would you leave this part in or cut it? Why have some directors chosen to cut it? Why do other directors choose to include it?

27   *In happy time*   you have come at just the right moment

30   *make bold*   taken the liberty

31   *suit*   appeal

33   *presently*   at once

3:1   *Enter* CASSIO *and* MUSICIANS

CASSIO   Masters, play here – I will content your pains –
              Something that's brief, and bid 'Good morrow, General'.

                                                              [*They play*

                              Enter CLOWN

CLOWN   Why, masters, have your instruments been in Naples, that they
              speak i' the nose thus?

FIRST MUSCIAN How, sir? How?   5

CLOWN   Are these, I pray you, wind instruments?

FIRST MUSCIAN Ay, marry are they, sir.

CLOWN   Oh, thereby hangs a tale.

FIRST MUSCIAN Whereby hangs a tale, sir?

CLOWN   Marry, sir, by many a wind instrument that I know. But, Masters,   10
              here's money for you, and the General so likes your music that he
              desires you, for love's sake, to make no more noise with it.

FIRST MUSCIAN Well, sir, we will not.

CLOWN   If you have any music that may not be heard, to 't again. But, as
              they say, to hear music the General does not greatly care.   15

FIRST MUSCIAN We have none such, sir.

CLOWN   Then put up your pipes in your bag, for I'll away. Go, vanish into
              air. Away!

                                                      [*Exeunt* MUSICIANS

CASSIO   Dost thou hear, mine honest friend?

CLOWN   No, I hear not your honest friend; I hear you.   20

CASSIO   Prithee keep up thy quillets. There's a poor piece of gold for thee –
              if the gentlewoman that attends the General's wife be stirring, tell her
              there's one Cassio entreats her a little favour of speech. Wilt thou do
              this?

CLOWN   She is stirring, sir; if she will stir hither, I shall seem to notify unto   25
              her.   [*Exit*

                              Enter IAGO

CASSIO   In happy time, Iago.

IAGO   You have not been abed then?

CASSIO   Why, no – the day had broke before we parted.
              I have made bold, Iago,   30
              To send in to your wife; my suit to her
              Is that she will to virtuous Desdemona
              Procure me some access.

IAGO   I'll send her to your presently;
              And I'll devise a mean to draw the Moor

37 a *Florentine more kind and honest* Cassio is from Florence and Iago is from Venice. Cassio means that not even a Florentine could be more kind and honest than Iago.

Cassio has already been taking steps to regain his position. When he reveals to Iago that he has already approached Emilia, does Iago show any surprise, or concealed annoyance, or might he know already?

39 *displeasure* being out of favour

41 *stoutly* wholeheartedly

42 *he you hurt* i.e. Montano

43 *great affinity* has important connections. *in wholesome wisdom* it was sensible to

44 *He might not but* he had no choice but to. *refuse* dismiss. *protests* insists

46 *by the front* directly

47 *bring you in* reinstate you

52 *bosom* inner thoughts and feelings

Compare Iago's willingness to send Emilia to Cassio and to get Othello out of the way with the next stage of his plan which he revealed at the end of Act 2 Scene 3.

Cassio has enlisted the help of Emilia and is arranging a meeting with Desdemona. Iago appears to be helping by getting Othello out of the way.

3:2

Othello assumes his public duties as Governor of Cyprus, inspecting the fortifications and sending letters to the Senate. Iago is now acting as his trusty deputy.

2 *do my duties* pay my respects

3 *works* fortifications

4 *Repair* return. *Well* very well

Although very short, scenes such as this help to create the impression of rapidly moving action. What kind of scenery, props or backdrop would you use to create the setting for this scene?

Look for other very short scenes in the play which serve a similar function. Try Act 2 Scene 2. Compare the functions these short scenes perform.

Although very short, there is strong dramatic irony in this scene. It is ironic that Othello should leave Desdemona to inspect the fortifications on the island just at the point when his personal life is about to come under attack.

        Out of the way, that your converse and business   35
        May be more free.

CASSIO   I humbly thank you for it.

                            [*Exit* IAGO

        I never knew a Florentine more kind and honest.

Enter EMILIA

EMILIA   Good morrow, good Lieutenant. I am sorry
        For your displeasure; but all will sure be well.
        The General and his wife are talking of it,   40
        And she speaks for you stoutly. The Moor replies
        That he you hurt is of great fame in Cyprus,
        And great affinity; and that in wholesome wisdom
        He might not but refuse you. But he protests he loves you,
        And needs no other suitor but his likings   45
        To take the safest occasion by the front
        To bring you in again.

CASSIO   Yet I beseech you,
        If you think fit, or that it may be done,
        Give me advantage of some brief discourse
        With Desdemon alone.

EMILIA   Pray you come in.   50
        I will bestow you where you shall have time
        To speak your bosom freely.

CASSIO   I am much bound to you.

                          [*Exeunt*

3:2

Enter OTHELLO, IAGO *and* GENTLEMEN

OTHELLO   These letters give, Iago, to the pilot,
        And by him do my duties to the Senate.
        That done, I will be walking on the works;
        Repair there to me.

IAGO   Well, my good lord, I'll do 't.   [*Exit*

OTHELLO   This fortification, gentlemen, shall we see 't?   5

GENTLEMEN   We'll wait upon your lordship.

                          [*Exeunt*

3:3

Desdemona assures Cassio that she will do everything she can to have him reinstated. Iago puts his plan to make Othello jealous into operation and its effects soon begin to become obvious. Othello becomes increasingly eaten away with jealousy at the thought of Desdemona with Cassio.

2 *All my abilities* all that I can

3 *warrant* promise

7 *bounteous* generous

12 *strangeness* estrangement

13 *politic* politically necessary

15 *nice* thin or insubstantial

16 *breed itself … circumstances* develop out of the circumstances

17 *supplied* filled

19 *doubt* fear

20 *warrant* guarantee

22 *article* detail

23 *watch him tame* keep him awake to tame him (Hawks were trained by keeping them awake.)

24 *board* meal table
      shrift confessional

26 *suit* appeal

27 *thy solicitor* the person who argues your case

28 *give thy cause away* give up on your case

34 *do your discretion* do what you think best

As Cassio sees Othello and Iago approaching from a distance, he decides to leave without being seen as he does not feel in the right frame of mind to meet Othello. He is seen though and immediately Iago begins to use this to his own advantage. Look at his comments in lines 36–9. These lines are designed to arouse Othello's suspicions. Often the lines are spoken as if Iago is thinking aloud. What tone of voice and facial expression and body movements could an actor use here. Does he frown? Rub his chin? Speak quietly as if to himself? How does Othello respond? Does he rise to the bait immediately or is he much more relaxed about Iago's comments, not believing that he has anything to worry about? Is there a point at which you think Othello's attitude may change?

3:3   *Enter* **Desdemona, Cassio** *and* **Emilia**

Desdemona Be thou assured, good Cassio, I will do
        All my abilities in thy behalf.

Emilia   Good madam, do. I warrant it grieves my husband
        As if the cause were his.

Desdemona Oh, that's an honest fellow! Do not doubt, Cassio,   5
        But I will have my lord and you again
        As friendly as you were.

Cassio   Bounteous madam,
        Whatever shall become of Michael Cassio,
        He's never anything but your true servant.

Desdemona I know 't; I thank you. You do love my lord,   10
        You have known him long, and be you well assured
        He shall in strangeness stand no farther off
        Than in a politic distance.

Cassio   Ay, but, lady,
        That policy may either last so long,
        Or feed upon such nice and waterish diet,   15
        Or breed itself so out of circumstances,
        That, I being absent, and my place supplied,
        My General will forget my love and service.

Desdemona Do not doubt that. Before Emilia here,
        I give thee warrant of thy place. Assure thee,   20
        If I do vow a friendship, I'll perform it
        To the last article. My lord shall never rest:
        I'll watch him tame and talk him out of patience;
        His bed shall seem a school, his board a shrift;
        I'll intermingle everything he does   25
        With Cassio's suit. Therefore be merry, Cassio,
        For thy solicitor shall rather die
        Than give thy cause away.

                    Enter **Othello** *and* **Iago** *at a distance*

Emilia   Madam, here comes my lord.

Cassio   Madam, I'll take my leave.   30

Desdemona Why, stay and hear me speak.

Cassio   Madam, not now – I am very ill at ease,
        Unfit for mine own purposes.

Desdemona Well, do your discretion.   [Exit **Cassio**

Iago   Ha! I like not that.

Othello   What dost thou say?   35

Iago   Nothing, my lord; or if – I know not what.

42   *suitor* someone pleading a case

43   *languishes* wasting away

46   *grace* favour

47   *present reconciliation take* take his immediate attempt to make peace

49   *in cunning* knowingly

52   *humbled* ashamed

63   *he's penitent* he's sorry for what he has done

64   *trespass* fault
     in our common reason in the normal way of thinking

65–6   *Save that … best* except in wartime even the best must sometimes be made an example of

66–7   *is not almost … private check* hardly worth even a private reprimand

70   *mammering* hesitating

72   *dispraisingly* critically

74   *To bring him in* to reinstate him

OTHELLO   Was not that Cassio parted from my wife?

IAGO   Cassio, my lord? No, sure, I cannot think it,
That he would steal away so guilty-like,
Seeing your coming.

OTHELLO   I do believe 'twas he.   40

DESDEMONA [*Approaching them*] How now, my lord?
I have been talking with a suitor here,
A man that languishes in your displeasure.

OTHELLO   Who is 't you mean?

DESDEMONA Why, your Lieutenant, Cassio. Good my lord,   45
If I have any grace or power to move you,
His present reconciliation take.
For if he be not one that truly loves you,
That errs in ignorance, and not in cunning,
I have no judgment in an honest face.   50
I prithee call him back.

OTHELLO   Went he hence now?

DESDEMONA Yes, faith; so humbled
That he hath left part of his grief with me
To suffer with him. Good love, call him back.

OTHELLO   Not now, sweet Desdemon; some other time.   55

DESDEMONA But shall 't be shortly?

OTHELLO   The sooner, sweet, for you.

DESDEMONA Shall 't be tonight, at supper?

OTHELLO   No, not tonight.

DESDEMONA Tomorrow dinner, then?

OTHELLO   I shall not dine at home;
I meet the captains at the citadel.

DESDEMONA Why then, tomorrow night; on Tuesday morn;   60
On Tuesday noon, or night, on Wednesday morn –
I prithee name the time, but let it not
Exceed three days. In faith, he's penitent;
And yet his trespass, in our common reason –
Save that, they say, the wars must make example   65
Out of the best – is not almost a fault
To incur a private check. When shall he come?
Tell me, Othello. I wonder in my soul
What you would ask me that I should deny
Or stand so mammering on! What? Michael Cassio,   70
That came a-wooing with you? And so many a time –
When I have spoke of you dispraisingly –
Hath ta'en your part, to have so much to do
To bring him in? By'r Lady, I could do much –

76   *boon* favour

> *Desdemona unwittingly plays into Iago's hands by pressing Cassio's case so persistently. How does she approach Othello? Does she laugh and try to make light of it? Does she pull at his sleeve? Her approach is certainly direct and this might emphasise her innocent and straightforward nature.*

79   *sue to* plead with

79–80   *a peculiar profit / To your own person* something to your own personal advantage

80   *suit* request

81   *touch* test

82   *poise and difficult weight* serious and problematical

83   *fearful* uncertain

84   *Whereon* having agreed as

88   *fancies* desired

> *Othello's response* **I will deny thee nothing** *suggests he has misunderstood the basis of Desdemona's plea. She goes on to explain that she is not asking for something for herself but is arguing for a course of action that is in Othello's own interest. Throughout this section, does he really listen to her or is he simply humouring her?*

90   *wretch* meant here to express affection

90–1   *Perdition … love thee* may my soul be damned if I do not love you

91–2   *And when … come again* and if ever I stop loving you it will be the end of the world

> *Look at Iago's questions and Othello's response in lines 93–107. It has often been said that these lines, as well as presenting dialogue, act as a set of stage directions to the actor playing Iago? How should the actor respond?*

99   *went between us* acted as a go-between

101   *Discern'st thou aught* do you see anything

102   *honest* trustworthy

106   *some monster* something terrible

OTHELLO	Prithee no more. Let him come when he will.	**75**
	I will deny thee nothing.	

DESDEMONA Why, this is not a boon;
'Tis as I should entreat you wear your gloves,
Or feed on nourishing dishes, or keep you warm,
Or sue to you to do a peculiar profit
To your own person. Nay, when I have a suit   **80**
Wherein I mean to touch your love indeed,
It shall be full of poise and difficult weight,
And fearful to be granted.

OTHELLO I will deny thee nothing.
Whereon, I do beseech thee, grant me this:
To leave me but a little to myself.   **85**

DESDEMONA Shall I deny you? No! Farewell, my lord.

OTHELLO Farewell, my Desdemona; I'll come to thee straight.

DESDEMONA Emilia, come. [*To* **OTHELLO**] Be as your fancies teach you;
Whate'er you be, I am obedient.

[*Exeunt* **DESDEMONA** *and* **EMILIA**

OTHELLO Excellent wretch! Perdition catch my soul   **90**
But I do love thee! And when I love thee not
Chaos is come again.

IAGO My noble lord –

OTHELLO What dost thou say, Iago?

IAGO Did Michael Cassio,
When you wooed my lady, know of your love?

OTHELLO He did, from first to last. Why dost thou ask?   **95**

IAGO But for a satisfaction of my thought –
No further harm.

OTHELLO Why of thy thought, Iago?

IAGO I did not think he had been acquainted with her.

OTHELLO Oh yes, and went between us very oft.

IAGO Indeed?   **100**

OTHELLO Indeed? Ay, indeed. Discern'st thou aught in that?
Is he not honest?

IAGO Honest, my lord?

OTHELLO Honest? Ay, honest!

IAGO My lord, for aught I know.

OTHELLO What dost thou think?

IAGO Think, my lord?

OTHELLO Think, my lord? By heaven, thou echoest me   **105**
As if there were some monster in thy thought

110	*of my counsel* in my confidence
112	*contract and purse thy brow together* frown
114	*conceit* idea
119	*stops* hesitations
121	*tricks of custom* typical plays
122–3	*close dilations … rule* secret feelings from the heart that cannot be controlled
126	*those that … seemed none* those that are not honest should not seem to be so
131	*ruminate* think things over
134	*I am … free to* even slaves are free to keep their thoughts to themselves
135	*say* suppose
136	*As where's* for example
138	*uncleanly apprehensions* corrupt thoughts
139	*leets* days when the courts are sitting *in sessions sit* sit in judgement
140	*meditation lawful* decent thoughts
142	*but think'st* suspect
142–3	*make'st … thy thoughts* keep your suspicions a secret from him
144	*I perchance am vicious in my guess* perhaps I am wrong in my understanding of the situation
145–6	*my natures … abuses* it is a flaw in my character to be suspicious

       Too hideous to be shown. Thou dost mean something.
       I heard thee say even now, thou lik'st not that,
       When Cassio left my wife: what didst not like?
       And when I told thee he was of my counsel   **110**
       In my whole course of wooing, thou criedst, 'Indeed?'
       And didst contract and purse thy brow together
       As if thou then hadst shut up in thy brain
       Some horrible conceit. If thou dost love me,
       Show me thy thought.   **115**

IAGO   My lord, you know I love you.

OTHELLO   I think thou dost;
       And, for I know thou art full of love and honesty,
       And weighest thy words before thou giv'st them breath,
       Therefore these stops of thine fright me the more;
       For such things in a false disloyal knave   **120**
       Are tricks of custom, but in a man that's just
       They are close dilations working from the heart
       That passion cannot rule.

IAGO   For Michael Cassio,
       I dare be sworn, I think that he is honest.

OTHELLO   I think so too.

IAGO   Men should be what they seem;   **125**
       Or those that be not, would they might seem none!

OTHELLO   Certain, men should be what they seem.

IAGO   Why then, I think Cassio's an honest man.

OTHELLO   Nay, yet there's more in this!
       I prithee speak to me as to thy thinkings,   **130**
       As thou dost ruminate, and give thy worst of thoughts
       The worst of words.

IAGO   Good my lord, pardon me.
       Though I am bound to every act of duty,
       I am not bound to that all slaves are free to.
       Utter my thoughts? Why, say they are vile and false –   **135**
       As where's that palace whereinto foul things
       Sometimes intrude not? Who has that breast so pure
       But some uncleanly apprehensions
       Keep leets and law-days, and in sessions sit
       With meditations lawful?   **140**

OTHELLO   Thou dost conspire against thy friend, Iago,
       If thou but think'st him wronged, and mak'st his ear
       A strange to thy thoughts.

IAGO   I do beseech you,
       Though I perchance am vicious in my guess –
       As I confess it is my nature's plague   **145**

146 *jealousy* suspicion

> In line 146 Iago introduces the word 'jealousy' into the conversation for the first time but he also makes himself sound hesitant and reluctant to speak his mind. He does this partly by speaking in long sentences which he sometimes breaks off from, leaving the phrase unfinished. Look at lines 143–53 and find where he does this.

147 *Shapes* imagines
wisdom good sense

148 *imperfectly conceits* mistakenly imagines

150 *scattering* random

151 *quiet* peace of mind

155 *immediate jewel* most treasured possession

158 *filches* steals

162 *custody* control

165 *cuckold* a man whose wife is unfaithful to him

166 *certain of his fate, loves not his wronger* knows that his wife deceives him and so stops loving her

168 *dotes* is infatuated
fondly foolishly

171 *fineless* unlimited

172 *ever* always

176–7 *follow still … suspicions* continually find new suspicions with every change of the moon

Iago (Ian McKellen) begins to work on Othello (Willard White) in the 1989 RSC production

177–8 *To be once in doubt / Is once to be resolved* once I doubt my wife's fidelity I will immediately find out the truth

179 *turn the business of my soul* focus my mind on

180 *exsufflicate and blown surmises* exaggerated and inflated imaginings

181 *Matching thy inference* such as you describe

185–6 *Nor from … revolt* nor will doubt her faithfulness because I feel that I do not deserve her

186 *doubt* suspect
revolt unfaithfulness

To spy into abuses, and oft my jealousy
Shapes faults that are not – that your wisdom
From one that so imperfectly conceits
Would take no notice, nor build yourself a trouble
Out of his scattering and unsure observance.   150
It were not for your quiet nor your good,
Nor for my manhood, honesty, and wisdom,
To let you know my thoughts.

OTHELLO   What dost thou mean?

IAGO   Good name in man and woman, dear my lord,
Is the immediate jewel of their souls.   155
Who steals my purse steals trash; 'tis something, nothing;
'Twas mine, 'tis his, and has been slave to thousands;
But he that filches from me my good name
Robs me of that which not enriches him
And makes me poor indeed.

OTHELLO   By heaven, I'll know thy thoughts!   160

IAGO   You cannot, if my heart were in your hand,
Nor shall not, whilst 'tis in my custody.

OTHELLO   Ha?

IAGO   Oh beware, my lord, of jealousy!
It is the green-eyed monster, which doth mock
The meat it feeds on. That cuckold lives in bliss   165
Who, certain of his fate, loves not his wronger;
But oh, what damnèd minutes tells he o'er
Who dotes yet doubts, suspects yet fondly loves!

OTHELLO   Oh misery!

IAGO   Poor and content is rich, and rich enough;   170
But riches fineless is as poor as winter
To him that ever fears he shall be poor.
Good God, the souls of all my tribe defend
From jealousy!

OTHELLO   Why? Why is this?
Think'st thou I'd make a life of jealousy,   175
To follow still the changes of the moon
With fresh suspicions? No. To be once in doubt
Is once to be resolved. Exchange me for a goat
When I shall turn the business of my soul
To such exsufflicate and blown surmises,   180
Matching thy inference. 'Tis not to make me jealous
To say my wife is fair, feeds well, loves company,
Is free of speech, sings, plays, and dances:
Where virtue is, these are more virtuous.
Nor from mine own weak merits will I draw   185
The smallest fear or doubt of her revolt,

193 *as I am bound* since it is my duty

194 *Receive* hear

196 *Wear your eyes thus* keep you eyes open
secure excessively trustful

197 *free* generous

198 *self-bounty* natural generosity

199 *our country disposition* they way our people behave (implying
the sexual behaviour of Venetian women)

201 *their best conscience* their highest moral ideal

> *Iago's words are intended to raise further doubts in Othello's mind and to remind him that Desdemona has already deceived a loved one once and might do it again. What kind of response does this provoke from Othello? In the 1995 film version, Laurence Fishburne playing Othello smiles at Iago's (played by Kenneth Brannagh) words, as if remembering his secret courtship of Desdemona. In some performances, though, it visibly increases the doubt in his mind. If you were playing the part of Othello, how would you respond at this point?*

206 *go to then* there you are then

207 *seeming* deceptive appearance

208 *seel her father's eyes up* make her father blind
(a falconry term – hawks were sometimes blindfolded for training)
oak a tightly grained wood

211 *bound* in debt

> *How would Iago say* **I see this hath a little dashed your spirits**? *Could it be a comic line?*

216 *strain* exaggerate

217 *grosser issues* more shocking conclusions (to do with sex)
larger reach wider implications

220 *vile success* deplorable consequences

221 *my thoughts aimed not* which I did not intend

223 *I do not think but* I am certain that

For she had eyes, and chose me. No, Iago,
I'll see before I doubt; when I doubt, prove;
And on the proof, there is no more but this:
Away at once with love or jealousy. 190

IAGO I am glad of this; for now I shall have reason
To show the love and duty that I bear you
With franker spirit. Therefore, as I am bound,
Receive it from me. I speak not yet of proof.
Look to your wife; observe her well with Cassio; 195
Wear your eyes thus: not jealous nor secure.
I would not have your free and noble nature,
Out of self-bounty, be abused. Look to 't.
I know our country disposition well –
In Venice they do let God see the pranks 200
They dare not show their husbands; their best conscience
Is not to leave 't undone, but keep 't unknown.

OTHELLO Dost thou say so?

IAGO She did deceive her father, marrying you;
And when she seemed to shake and fear your looks, 205
She loved them most.

OTHELLO And so she did.

IAGO Why, go to then.
She that, so young, could give out such a seeming
To seel her father's eyes up, close as oak –
He thought 'twas witchcraft. – But I am much to blame.
I humbly do beseech you of your pardon 210
For too much loving you.

OTHELLO I am bound to thee for ever.

IAGO I see this hath a little dashed your spirits.

OTHELLO Not a jot, not a jot.

IAGO I' faith I fear it has.
I hope you will consider what is spoke
Comes from my love. But I do see you're moved. 215
I am to pray you not to strain my speech
To grosser issues, nor to larger reach
Than to suspicion.

OTHELLO I will not.

IAGO Should you do so, my lord,
My speech should fall into such vile success 220
Which my thoughts aimed not. Cassio's my worthy friend –
My lord, I see you're moved.

OTHELLO No, not much moved.
I do not think but Desdemona's honest.

IAGO Long live she so – and long live you to think so!

225	*nature erring from itself* someone can act out of character
227	*affect* look favourably on
	proposèd matches proposals of marriage
228	*clime* country
	complexion, and degree nature and status
230	*a will most rank* a most corrupt intention
231	*Foul disproportion* disgusting perversion
232–3	*in position / Distinctly* specifically
234	*recoiling* returning
235	*fall* happen
	match compare
	country forms good looking men from her own country
236	*happily* perhaps
243	*scan* investigate
246	*hold him off* keep him at a distance
248	*strain his entertainment* pleads for his reinstatement
249	*vehement importunity* powerful appeals
251	*busy* interfering
253	*hold her free* think of her as innocent
254	*government* self-control
256	*qualities* kinds of people
	with a learnèd spirit with much experience
257	*prove* find
	haggard wanton (a falconry term to describe a wild hawk)
258	*jesses* leather straps attached to a hawk's legs to prevent it escaping
259	*whistle her off* let her fly off
	let her down the wind let her fly free to wherever she wants
260	*prey at fortune* fend for herself
	Haply perhaps
261–2	*soft parts … chamberers have* elegant social skills possessed by courtiers (ladies' men)
264	*abused* deceived

OTHELLO	And yet, how nature erring from itself –	225

IAGO Ay, there's the point; as, to be bold with you,
Not to affect many proposèd matches
Of her own clime, complexion, and degree,
Whereto we see in all things nature tends –
Foh! One may smell in such a will most rank, 230
Foul disproportion, thoughts unnatural.
But pardon me – I do not in position
Distinctly speak of her, though I may fear
Her will, recoiling to her better judgment,
May fall to match you with her country forms, 235
And happily repent.

OTHELLO Farewell, farewell.
If more thou dost perceive, let me know more.
Set on thy wife to observe. Leave me, Iago.

IAGO [*Going*] My lord, I take my leave.

OTHELLO Why did I marry? This honest creature doubtless 240
Sees and knows more, much more, than he unfolds.

IAGO [*Returning*] My lord, I would I might entreat your honour
To scan this thing no farther. Leave it to time.
Although 'tis fit that Cassio have his place,
For sure he fills it up with great ability, 245
Yet if you please to hold him off awhile,
You shall by that perceive him and his means.
Note if your lady strain his entertainment
With any strong or vehement importunity –
Much will be seen in that. In the mean time 250
Let me be thought too busy in my fears,
As worthy cause I have to fear I am,
And hold her free, I do beseech your honour.

OTHELLO Fear not my government.

IAGO   I once more take my leave.   [*Exit*

OTHELLO This fellow's of exceeding honesty, 255
And knows all qualities, with a learnèd spirit
Of human dealings. If I do prove her haggard,
Though that her jesses were my dear heart-strings,
I'd whistle her off, and let her down the wind
To prey at fortune. Haply, for I am black 260
And have not those soft parts of conversation
That chamberers have, or for I am declined
Into the vale of years – yet that's not much –
She's gone: I am abused, and my relief
Must be to loathe her. Oh curse of marriage, 265
That we can call these delicate creatures ours,
And not their appetites! I had rather be a toad

268   *vapour* stinking air

270   *the plague to great ones* i.e. having an unfaithful wife

271   *Prerogatived … base* they are less privileged than men of lower status (i.e. Men of high status are more likely to have unfaithful wives than common men.)

272   *destiny unshunnable* inevitable fate

273   *forkèd plague* cuckold's horns (It was believed that a cuckold grew horns which everyone could see but himself.)

274   *do quicken* are born

> *Which lines in Othello's soliloquy suggest that Iago's insinuations have shaken his faith in himself? What mood could Othello be in here – angry, sad, reflective – or does he show a mixture of emotions and swing from one to another?*

278   *attend* await

281   *pain* headache (also has the implication of the cuckold's horns)

282   *watching* staying awake

284   *napkin* handkerchief

> *This is the important moment where Desdemona drops her handkerchief and Emilia picks it up. The stage directions give a basic indication of what happens here but it is important that the audience are aware of the full significance of what is happening. If you were producing the play how would you handle this part of the scene? Where would the actors stand? What would they do? How would you arrange it so that the handkerchief could be dropped without Desdemona or the others noticing, while at the same time making sure that the audience were aware of it? Or doesn't it matter if the audience don't actually see it dropped?*

288   *remembrance* keepsake

289   *wayward* unpredictable

291   *conjured* solemnly promise

292   *reserves* keeps

294   *work ta'en out* the embroidery copied

296   *fantasy* whim

299   *thing* Emilia means the handkerchief, but Iago takes this as a reference for the female sexual organ.
        common insultingly implying it is available to everyone

And live upon the vapour of a dungeon
Than keep a corner in the thing I love
For others' uses. Yet 'tis the plague to great ones;   270
Prerogatived are they less than the base.
'Tis destiny unshunnable, like death –
Even then this forkèd plague is fated to us
When we do quicken. Look where she comes.

Enter DESDEMONA *and* EMILIA

If she be false, heaven mocked itself!   275
I'll not believe it.

DESDEMONA   How now, my dear Othello?
Your dinner, and the generous islanders
By you invited, do attend your presence.

OTHELLO   I am to blame.

DESDEMONA   Why do you speak so faintly?
Are you not well?   280

OTHELLO   I have a pain upon my forehead, here.

DESDEMONA Faith, that's with watching; 'twill away again.
Let me but bind it hard, within this hour
It will be well.   [*Tries to tie her handkerchief around his head*

OTHELLO   Your napkin is too little –
Let it alone. [*Pushes it away; it falls*] Come, I'll go in with you.   285

DESDEMONA I am very sorry that you are not well.

[*Exeunt* OTHELLO *and* DESDEMONA

EMILIA   I am glad I have found this napkin;
This was her first remembrance from the Moor;
My wayward husband hath a hundred times
Wooed me to steal it, but she loves so the token –   290
For he conjured her she should ever keep it –
That she reserves it evermore about her
To kiss and talk to.
I'll have the work ta'en out and give 't Iago.
What he will do with it heaven knows, not I –   295
I nothing, but to please his fantasy.

Enter IAGO

IAGO   How now, what do you here alone?

EMILIA   Do not you chide: I have a thing for you.

IAGO   You have a thing for me? It is a common thing –

EMILIA   Ha?   300

IAGO   To have a foolish wife.

EMILIA   Oh, is that all? What will you give me now
For that same handkerchief?

308	*negligence* accident
309	*to the advantage* by good luck
313	*import* importance
315	*Be not ackown on 't* say nothing about it

> *When Iago realises that Emilia has the handkerchief, he immediately sees how he can use it to his advantage. How might he respond when he realises that she has it? Does he simply snatch it from her? What other ways could this be played? In the 1985 RSC production Emila teased Iago with it in a sexually flirtatious way, brushing it passed his lips and he took it in his teeth. Does Shakespeare want us to see Emilia here as powerful, sexy and manipulative? Desperate for attention? Sadly struggling to get some response from her husband? Aware of the danger of what she is doing?*

318	*Trifles light as air* insignificant things
319	*confirmations* evidence
320	*Holy Writ* the Bible (believed to be completely true)
322	*conceits* fantasies
323	*distaste* taste unpleasant
324	*with a little* after a little while
325	*mines of sulphur* hell
326	*poppy* opium
	mandragora a narcotic
327	*drowsy syrups* sleeping potions
329	*owedst* owned
331	*Avaunt* go away
	set me on the rack torture me
332	*abused* deceived
336	*free* untroubled

IAGO		What handkerchief?
EMILIA	What handkerchief!	
	Why, that the Moor first gave to Desdemona –	305
	That which so often you did bid me steal.	
IAGO	Hast stol'n it from her?	
EMILIA	No, faith, she let it drop by negligence,	
	And, to the advantage, I being here took 't up.	
	Look, here it is.	
IAGO	A good wench, give it me.	310
EMILIA	What will you do with't, that you have been so earnest	
	To have me filch it?	
IAGO [*Snatching it*]	Why, what is that to you?	
EMILIA	If it be not for some purpose of import,	
	Give 't me again. Poor lady, she'll run mad	
	When she shall lack it.	
IAGO	Be not acknown on 't;	315
	I have use for it. Go, leave me.	

[*Exit* EMILIA

I will in Cassio's lodging lose this napkin
And let him find it. Trifles light as air
Are to the jealous confirmations strong
As proofs of Holy Writ. This may do something. 320
The Moor already changes with my poison –
Dangerous conceits are in their natures poisons,
Which at the first are scarce found to distaste,
But, with a little, act upon the blood,
Burn like the mines of sulphur.

Enter OTHELLO

I did say so. 325
Look where he comes! Not poppy, nor mandragora,
Nor all the drowsy syrups of the world,
Shall ever medicine thee to that sweet sleep
Which thou owedst yesterday.

OTHELLO	Ha! Ha! False to me?	
IAGO	Why, how now, General! No more of that.	330
OTHELLO	Avaunt! Be gone! Thou hast set me on the rack.	
	I swear 'tis better to be much abused	
	Than but to know't a little.	
IAGO	How now, my lord!	
OTHELLO	What sense had I of her stol'n hours of lust?	
	I saw 't not, thought it not, it harmed not me;	335
	I slept the next night well, fed well, was free and merry;	
	I found not Cassio's kisses on her lips.	

338	*wanting* missing
339	*Let him not know 't* as long as he doesn't know it
341	*general* whole
342	*Pioners* the trench diggers (i.e. the lowest rank of soldier)
343	*So* so long as
344	*tranquil mind* peace of mind
346	*That makes ambition virtue* that makes ambition a good thing
347	*trump* trumpet
349	*all quality* all the fine qualities (that war brings out)
350	*circumstance* pageantry
351	*mortal engines* deadly artillery
351–2	*rude throats … counterfeit* whose rough voices imitate the terrible thunder of Jove
353	*occupation* purpose in life
356	*ocular* visible

Iago has reached the point of no return. He has set doubts in Othello's mind to the extent that Othello is, in effect, saying that Iago must prove Desdemona is a whore or he will kill him. How could this be played to emphasise the danger that Iago himself is now in? In the 1985 RSC production, Othello, played by Ben Kingsley, grabbed Iago, played by David Suchet, by the throat at line 355 and didn't release him until line 369. In the 1995 film version, the scene is set on a beach and Othello grabs Iago and drags him into the sea, holding his head under water while threatening him. How would you do it?

361	*probation* proof
365	*all remorse* all thoughts of being sorry for doing wrong
371	*God b' wi' you* God be with you (i.e. goodbye)
	Oh wretched fool Iago is talking about himself here.
372	*vice* weakness
375	*profit* useful lesson
376	*sith* since
	breeds such offence is so dangerous

He that is robbed, not wanting what is stol'n,
Let him not know 't, and he's not robbed at all.

IAGO   I am sorry to hear this.   340

OTHELLO   I had been happy if the general camp,
Pioners and all, had tasted her sweet body,
So I had nothing known. Oh now, for ever
Farewell the tranquil mind! Farewell content!
Farewell the plumèd troops, and the big wars   345
That makes ambition virtue! Oh farewell,
Farewell the neighing steed and the shrill trump,
The spirit-stirring drum, the ear-piercing fife,
The royal banner, and all quality,
Pride, pomp and circumstance of glorious war!   350
And, oh you mortal engines, whose rude throats
The immortal Jove's dread clamours counterfeit,
Farewell! Othello's occupation's gone.

IAGO   Is 't possible, my lord?

OTHELLO   Villain, be sure thou prove my love a whore!   355
Be sure of it; give me the ocular proof;
Or, by the worth of mine eternal soul,
Thou hadst been better have been born a dog
Than answer my waked wrath.

IAGO   Is't come to this?

OTHELLO   Make me to see 't, or at the least so prove it   360
That the probation bear no hinge nor loop
To hang a doubt on – or woe upon thy life!

IAGO   My noble lord –

OTHELLO   If thou dost slander her and torture me,
Never pray more; abandon all remorse;   365
On horror's head horrors accumulate;
Do deeds to make heaven weep, all earth amazed;
For nothing canst thou to damnation add
Greater than that.

IAGO   Oh grace! Oh heaven forgive me!
Are you a man? Have you a soul? Or sense?   370
God b' wi' you; take mine office. Oh wretched fool,
That lov'st to make thine honesty a vice!
Oh monstrous world! Take note, take note, oh world:
To be direct and honest is not safe.
I thank you for this profit, and from hence   375
I'll love no friend, sith love breeds such offence.

OTHELLO   Nay, stay: thou shouldst be honest.

IAGO   I should be wise, for honesty's a fool
And loses that it works for.

382   *fresh* fair

383   *Dian's visage* the face of Diana, the goddess of chastity

386   *Would I were satisfied* I wish I had proof

389   *satisfied* convinced

> *Iago could be played in a variety of ways here. What do you think his response might be? He could respond angrily to this mistreatment or he might act as if emotionally very hurt, giving a sense that he has been unjustly treated simply for trying to help Othello.*

391   *supervisor* spectator. *grossly gape on* crudely watch

392   *behold her topped* watch a man having sex with her

Othello (Paul Robeson) and Iago (Sam Wanamaker) in the 1989 RSC production

> *What effect do these lines have on Othello? Would he beat his head? Fall to his knees? Cover his ears to shut out Iago's words?*

394   *prospect* situation

395   *bolster* share a pillow with someone

396   *More* others

399   *prime ... hot* sexually excited

400   *salt* lecherous. *in pride* on heat. *gross* crude

402   *imputation and strong circumstances* allegations and strong circumstantial evidence

405   *living* convincing

406   *office* task

408   *Pricked* spurred on

412   *loose of soul* unguarded about their inner thoughts

416   *gripe* grip

OTHELLO   By the world,
I think my wife be honest, and think she is not;   380
I think that thou art just, and think thou art not –
I'll have some proof. My name, that was as fresh
As Dian's visage, is now begrimed and black
As mine own face. If there be cords, or knives,
Poison, or fire, or suffocating streams,   385
I'll not endure it. Would I were satisfied!

IAGO   I see, sir, you are eaten up with passion.
I do repent me that I put it to you.
You would be satisfied?

OTHELLO   Would? Nay, and I will.

IAGO   And may. But how? How satisfied, my lord?   390
Would you, the supervisor, grossly gape on?
Behold her topped?

OTHELLO   Death and damnation! Oh!

IAGO   It were a tedious difficulty, I think,
To bring them to that prospect. Damn them then,
If ever mortal eyes do see them bolster   395
More than their own! What then? How then?
What shall I say? Where's satisfaction?
It is impossible you should see this,
Were they as prime as goats, as hot as monkeys,
As salt as wolves in pride, and fools as gross   400
As ignorance made drunk. But yet, I say,
If imputation and strong circumstances
Which lead directly to the door of truth
Will give you satisfaction, you might have 't.

OTHELLO   Give me a living reason she's disloyal.   405

IAGO   I do not like the office.
But sith I am entered in this cause so far –
Pricked to 't by foolish honesty and love –
I will go on. I lay with Cassio lately,
And being troubled with a raging tooth,   410
I could not sleep. There are a kind of men
So loose of soul, that in their sleeps will mutter
Their affairs. One of this kind is Cassio.
In sleep I heard him say, 'Sweet Desdemona,
Let us be wary, let us hide our loves!'   415
And then, sir, would he gripe and wring my hand,
Cry, 'Oh sweet creature!' then kiss me hard,
As if he plucked up kisses by the roots
That grew upon my lips; laid his leg o'er my thigh,
And sighed, and kissed, and then cried, 'Cursèd fate   420
That gave thee to the Moor!'

423 *foregone conclusion* that something has already happened

424 *shrewd doubt* strong suspicion

425 *thicken* confirm

437 *the slave* Cassio

440 *fond* foolish

443 *crown and hearted throne* sovereign of my heart

444 *fraught* burden

445 *aspics* asps (poisonous snakes)

> *What has happened to Othello's speech here? How could it be spoken by an actor to reveal his state of mind?*

448 *Pontic Sea* Black Sea

449 *compulsive* irresistible

451 *Propontic* Sea of Marmora
Hellespont The Dardanelles

454 *capable and wide* fitting and severe

455 *marble* hard and cold

457 *engage* pledge

458 *lights above* stars

459 *elements* earth, air, fire and water
clip surround

OTHELLO	Oh monstrous! Monstrous!
IAGO	Nay, this was but his dream.
OTHELLO	But this denoted a foregone conclusion,
	'Tis a shrewd doubt, though it be but a dream.
IAGO	And this may help to thicken other proofs
	That do demonstrate thinly.
OTHELLO	I'll tear her all to pieces!
IAGO	Nay, yet be wise. Yet we see nothing done;
	She may be honest yet. Tell me but this –
	Have you not sometimes seen a handkerchief,
	Spotted with strawberries, in your wife's hand?
OTHELLO	I gave her such a one; 'twas my first gift.
IAGO	I know not that, but such a handkerchief –
	I am sure it was your wife's – did I today
	See Cassio wipe his beard with.
OTHELLO	If it be that –
IAGO	If it be that, or any that was hers,
	It speaks against her with the other proofs.
OTHELLO	Oh that the slave had forty thousand lives!
	One is too poor, too weak for my revenge.
	Now do I see 'tis true. Look here, Iago:
	All my fond love thus do I blow to heaven –
	'Tis gone.
	Arise, black vengeance, from the hollow hell!
	Yield up, oh love, thy crown and hearted throne
	To tyrannous hate! Swell, bosom, with thy fraught,
	For 'tis of aspics' tongues!
IAGO	Yet be content.
OTHELLO	Oh blood! Blood! Blood!
IAGO	Patience, I say: your mind may change.
OTHELLO	Never, Iago. Like to the Pontic Sea,
	Whose icy current and compulsive course
	Ne'er feels retiring ebb, but keeps due on
	To the Propontic and the Hellespont,
	Even so my bloody thoughts with violent pace
	Shall ne'er look back, ne'er ebb to humble love,
	Till that a capable and wide revenge
	Swallow them up. Now by yond marble heaven,
	In the due reverence of a sacred vow
	I here engage my words.
IAGO	Do not rise yet.
	Witness, you ever-burning lights above,
	You elements that clip us round about,

Line numbers: 425, 430, 435, 440, 445, 450, 455

[*Kneels* (line 455)
[*Kneels*

461	*execution*	use
	wit	intelligence
464	*greet*	welcome
465	*vain*	empty
466	*put thee to 't*	take you up on it
468	*is dead*	is as good as dead
470	*lewd minx*	lecherous animal
472	*furnish me*	provide myself with
473	*fair devil*	i.e. Desdemona

Compare the way Othello speaks at the end of this scene with the way he speaks in Scene 1 of this Act. How has it changed? How does this change in speech reflect changes within Othello's mind and emotional state?

Iago has shaken Othello's faith in Desdemona and he has rapidly become convinced of her infidelity. Iago has Desdemona's handkerchief and is going to use it to further ensnare her and Cassio. By the end of this scene, Othello appears convinced of her unfaithfulness and gives Iago instructions to kill Cassio while he determines to kill Desdemona himself. Iago is promoted to Othello's lieutenant.

3:4

Desdemona is worried about the loss of her handkerchief. Othello enters trying to hide his disturbed state of mind and Desdemona begins to plead for Cassio. Othello asks her for the handkerchief but Desdemona tries to avoid the subject, pressing her plea for Cassio. Othello becomes angry and leaves. Cassio gives Desdemona's handkerchief, which he has found in his lodgings, to Bianca, a prostitute who has fallen in love with him.

1	*sirrah*	a way of addressing someone of lover status
2	*lies*	is lodging (The Clown plays on the word 'lie' in its sense of not telling the truth.)
4	*'tis stabbing*	it is a stabbing matter
6	*To tell … I lie*	if I were to tell you where Cassio is lodging I would be lying (because he doesn't know)
8	*devise*	invent
9	*in mine own throat*	to tell a blatant lie
10	*edified*	enlightened

	Witness that here Iago doth give up	460
	The execution of his wit, hands, heart,	
	To wronged Othello's service. Let him command,	
	And to obey shall be in me remorse,	
	What bloody business ever.	[*They rise*

OTHELLO   I greet thy love,
Not with vain thanks, but with acceptance bounteous,   465
And will upon the instant put thee to 't.
Within these three days let me hear thee say
That Cassio's not alive.

IAGO   My friend is dead.
'Tis done at your request. But let her live.

OTHELLO   Damn her, lewd minx! Oh, damn her! Damn her!   470
Come, go with me apart. I will withdraw
To furnish me with some swift means of death
For the fair devil. Now art thou my Lieutenant.

IAGO   I am your own for ever.   [*Exeunt*

3:4   *Enter* DESDEMONA, EMILIA *and a* CLOWN

DESDEMONA   Do you know, sirrah, where Lieutenant Cassio lies?

CLOWN   I dare not say he lies anywhere.

DESDEMONA   Why, man?

CLOWN   He's a soldier, and for one to say a soldier lies, 'tis stabbing.

DESDEMONA   Go to! Where lodges he?   5

CLOWN   To tell you where he lodges is to tell you where I lie.

DESDEMONA   Can anything be made of this?

CLOWN   I know not where he lodges, and for me to devise a lodging, and say
he lies here or he lies there, were to lie in mine own throat.

DESDEMONA   Can you inquire him out, and be edified by report?   10

11   *catechize* question

13   *moved* urged

15   *compass* range
     wit intelligence

> The scene opens with the reappearance of the Clown. Why do you think that Shakespeare included this brief interlude? Does it have any function dramatically on a performance? Could it be cut without detracting from the play?

17   *Where should I lose* where might I have lost

20   *crusadoes* a gold coin
     but if it were not for the fact that

21   *true* pure
     baseness unworthiness

25   *humours* moods

28   *Oh hardness to dissemble* how hard it is to keep up a pretence

> When Othello enters what kind of mood is he in? What is the significance of his aside **Oh hardness to dissemble!**? How could this be spoken? Sadly? Angrily? With bitterness? How does this contrast with his next line spoken aloud, **How do you do Desdemona?**?

30   *moist* a moist palm was said to indicate a lustful nature

32   *argues* suggests
     fruitfulness generosity (also fertile and suggests lust)
     liberal free and generous (hinting at being a bit too free sexually)

34   *sequester* separation
     liberty freedom

35   *castigation* punishment
     exercise devout act of worship

38   *frank* open and honest

41–2 *The hearts … not hearts* in the old days, lovers gave their hands to each other as a sign that they gave their hearts, but these days you cannot trust that because they give their hands they also give their hearts

43   *I cannot speak of this* Desdemona can say nothing because she does not follow what Othello is talking about.

44   *chuck* a term of affection

46   *salt and sorry rheum* a heavy running cold (salt also has connotations of lecherousness)

CLOWN   I will catechize the world for him; that is, make questions, and by
        them answer.

DESDEMONA Seek him; bid him come hither; tell him I have moved my lord on
        his behalf, and hope all will be well.

CLOWN   To do this is within the compass of man's wit, and therefore I will   15
        attempt the doing of it.

                                                              [*Exit*

DESDEMONA Where should I lose the handkerchief, Emilia?

EMILIA   I know not, madam.

DESDEMONA Believe me, I had rather have lost my purse
        Full of crusadoes – and, but my noble Moor   20
        Is true of mind, and made of no such baseness
        As jealous creatures are, it were enough
        To put him to ill-thinking.

EMILIA   Is he not jealous?

DESDEMONA Who, he? I think the sun where he was born
        Drew all such humours from him.

EMILIA   Look where he comes.   25

                       Enter OTHELLO

DESDEMONA I will not leave him now till Cassio
        Be called to him. How is it with you, my lord?

OTHELLO   Well, my good lady. [*Aside*] Oh hardness to dissemble!
        [*Aloud*] How do you, Desdemona?

DESDEMONA   Well, my good lord.

OTHELLO   Give me your hand. This hand is moist, my lady.   30

DESDEMONA It hath felt no age nor known no sorrow.

OTHELLO   This argues fruitfulness, and liberal heart –
        Hot, hot, and moist. This hand of yours requires
        A sequester from liberty; fasting and prayer;
        Much castigation; exercise devout;   35
        For here's a young and sweating devil here
        That commonly rebels. 'Tis a good hand,
        A frank one.

DESDEMONA You may indeed say so,
        For 'twas that hand that gave away my heart.   40

OTHELLO   A liberal hand! The hearts of old gave hands,
        But our new heraldry is hands, not hearts.

DESDEMONA I cannot speak of this. Come now, your promise!

OTHELLO   What promise, chuck?

DESDEMONA I have sent to bid Cassio come speak with you.   45

OTHELLO   I have a salt and sorry rheum offends me;

52 *charmer* magician

54 *amiable* lovable

54–5 *subdue my father / Entirely to her love* make my father love her completely

57 *hold her loathèd* hate her
spirits emotions

58 *fancies* loves

61 *darling* precious possession

62 *perdition* damnation

64 *web* weave

65 *sibyl* prophetess

65–6 *that had … compasses* who had lived for two hundred years

67 *fury* frenzied trance

68 *worms* silkworms
hallowed holy

69 *mummy* a liquid derived from embalmed bodies supposed to possess magical properties

70 *Conserved of* prepared from

72 *veritable* true

74 *startingly* disjointedly
rash wildly

75 *out o' the way* lost

77 *an if* if

Lend me thy handkerchief.

DESDEMONA   Here, my lord.

OTHELLO   That which I gave you.

DESDEMONA   I have it not about me.

OTHELLO   Not?

DESDEMONA   No indeed, my lord.

OTHELLO   Not?   That is a fault.   50
That handkerchief
Did an Egyptian to my mother give;
She was a charmer, and could almost read
The thoughts of people. She told her, while she kept it
'Twould make her amiable, and subdue my father
Entirely to her love; but if she lost it   55
Or made a gift of it, my father's eye
Should hold her loathèd, and his spirits should hunt
After new fancies. She, dying, gave it me
And bid me, when my fate would have me wived,
To give it her. I did so; and take heed on 't –   60
Make it a darling, like your precious eye.
To lose 't or give 't away, were such perdition
As nothing else could match.

DESDEMONA   Is 't possible?

OTHELLO   'Tis true: there's magic in the web of it.
A sibyl that had numbered in the world   65
The sun to course two hundred compasses
In her prophetic fury sewed the work;
The worms were hallowed that did breed the silk;
And it was dyed in mummy, which the skilful
Conserved of maidens' hearts.

DESDEMONA   I' faith, is 't true?   70

OTHELLO   Most veritable. Therefore look to 't well.

DESDEMONA Then would to God that I had never seen it!

OTHELLO   Ha! Wherefore?

DESDEMONA Why do you speak so startingly and rash?

OTHELLO   Is 't lost? Is 't gone? Speak, is it out o' the way?   75

DESDEMONA Heaven bless us!

OTHELLO   Say you?

DESDEMONA   It is not lost.
But what an if it were?

OTHELLO   How!

DESDEMONA I say it is not lost.

OTHELLO   Fetch 't, let me see it!

80	*put me from* distract me from
82	*My mind misgives* I'm worried about this
84	*sufficient* capable
85	*talk me* talk to me

> *Othello's focus in these lines has been on the handkerchief. How has Desdemona handled the situation? What kind of body language do you think she and Othello show here? Does she show fear? How could she show this? Why does she lie about the handkerchief?*

93	*unhappy in* unfortunate in
94	*'Tis not a year or two shows us a man* it takes more than a year or two to know what a man is really like
95	*all but* only
99	*importune her* plead with her
103	*Exist* be valued *member of* share in
104	*office* duty
106	*mortal* unforgivable
108	*purposed merit in futurity* the good things I intend to do in the future
109	*ransom me* win me back
110	*But ... benefit* even to know this would help me
111	*clothe me in a forced content* put on an outward appearance of accepting the situation
112–13	*shut myself ... fortune's alms* commit myself to some other way of life and take whatever fate sends my way
114	*advocation* appeal *in tune* appropriate

DESDEMONA Why, so I can; but I will not now.
This is a trick to put me from my suit. 80
Pray you, let Cassio be received again.

OTHELLO Fetch me the handkerchief. My mind misgives –

DESDEMONA Come, come!
You'll never meet a more sufficient man.

OTHELLO The handkerchief!

DESDEMONA I pray, talk me of Cassio – 85

OTHELLO The handkerchief!

DESDEMONA A man that all his time
Hath founded his good fortunes on your love,
Shared dangers with you –

OTHELLO The handkerchief!

DESDEMONA I' faith, you are to blame.

OTHELLO Zounds! [*Exit* 90

EMILIA Is not this man jealous?

DESDEMONA I ne'er saw this before.
Sure there's some wonder in this handkerchief;
I am most unhappy in the loss of it.

EMILIA 'Tis not a year or two shows us a man.
They are all but stomachs, and we all but food; 95
They eat us hungerly, and when they are full
They belch us. Look you, Cassio and my husband.

Enter IAGO *and* CASSIO

IAGO There is no other way; 'tis she must do it.
And lo the happiness! Go and importune her.

DESDEMONA How now, good Cassio? What's the news with you? 100

CASSIO Madam, my former suit. I do beseech you
That by your virtuous means I may again
Exist, and be a member of his love
Whom I, with all the office of my heart,
Entirely honour. I would not be delayed. 105
If my offence be of such mortal kind
That nor my service past, nor present sorrows,
Nor purposed merit in futurity,
Can ransom me into his love again,
But to know so must be my benefit; 110
So shall I clothe me in a forced content,
And shut myself up in some other course
To fortune's alms.

DESDEMONA Alas, thrice-gentle Cassio,
My advocation is not now in tune:

123

116 *in favour, as in humour, altered* as much changed in appearance as he is in mood

117 *sanctified* holy

119 *within the blank* at the centre of the target

121–2 *and more … dare* I will do more for you than I would dare to do for myself

> It is obviously no surprise to Iago that Othello is angry and his question **Is my lord angry?** is full of irony. How might he say this? With mild surprise? Shock? Puzzlement? Disbelief? Sympathy?

125–8 *I have seen … own brother* I have seen cannons blast rows of his soldiers into pieces and even blow away the man standing next to him (he still remained calm even under such circumstances)

129 *something of moment then* this must be something of great importance

130 *There's matter in 't* it must be important

132 *unhatched practice* secret plot

133 *Made demonstrable* disclosed

134 *puddled* muddied

135 *wrangle* argue

136 *object* concern

137 *endues* leads

138 *members* limbs

140 *observancy* attention

141 *bridal* wedding day
Beshrew me much I am to blame

140 *unhandsome* inadequate

143 *Arraigning* accusing

144 *suborned the witness* given false evidence

145 *indicted* charged

146 *conception* silly idea

147 *toy* whim

150 *not ever* not always
for the cause for a good reason

152 *Begot upon itself, born on itself* self-perpetuating

My lord is not my lord; nor should I know him   **115**
Were he in favour, as in humour, altered.
So help me every spirit sanctified
As I have spoken for you all my best,
And stood within the blank of his displeasure
For my free speech. You must awhile be patient.   **120**
What I can do, I will; and more I will
Than for myself I dare. Let that suffice you.

IAGO   Is my lord angry?

EMILIA   He went hence but now,
And certainly in strange unquietness.

IAGO   Can he be angry? I have seen the cannon   **125**
When it hath blown his ranks into the air,
And, like the devil, from his very arm
Puffed his own brother – and is he angry?
Something of moment then. I will go meet him.
There's matter in 't indeed if he be angry.   **130**

DESDEMONA I prithee do so.

                                                    [*Exit* IAGO

                          Something, sure, of state,
Either from Venice, or some unhatched practice
Made demonstrable here in Cyprus to him,
Hath puddled his clear spirit; and in such cases
Men's natures wrangle with inferior things,   **135**
Though great ones are their object. 'Tis even so.
For let our finger ache, and it endues
Our other healthful members even to a sense
Of pain. Nay, we must think men are not gods,
Nor of them look for such observancy   **140**
As fits the bridal. Beshrew me much, Emilia,
I was – unhandsome warrior as I am –
Arraigning his unkindness with my soul;
But now I find I had suborned the witness,
And he's indicted falsely.

EMILIA   Pray heaven it be   **145**
State matters, as you think, and no conception
Nor no jealous toy concerning you.

DESDEMONA Alas the day, I never gave him cause.

EMILIA   But jealous souls will not be answered so;
They are not ever jealous for the cause,   **150**
But jealous for they're jealous. It is a monster
Begot upon itself, born on itself.

DESDEMONA Heaven keep the monster from Othello's mind!

EMILIA   Lady, amen.

156 *fit* ready to listen
move your suit plead your case

157 *effect it* make it successful

159 *'Save you* God save you

163 *What, keep a week away?* Why have you been away for a week?

164 *Eight score eight* a hundred and sixty-eight

168 *continuate* uninterrupted

169 *Strike off this score* settle this debt

170 *Take me this work out* copy this embroidery for me

171 *token* love-token
newer friend another mistress

176 *remembrance* gift

179 *demanded* claimed

What is the irony in Bianca's reaction to the handkerchief? How might she respond to make this irony more explicit to the audience?

183 *attend here on* wait for

184 *no addition* not to my advantage

185 *womaned* with a woman

DESDEMONA I will go seek him. Cassio, walk here about. 155
        If I do find him fit, I'll move your suit
        And seek to effect it to my uttermost.

CASSIO   I humbly thank your ladyship.

                             [*Exeunt* **DESDEMONA** *and* **EMILIA**

                Enter **BIANCA**

BIANCA   'Save you, friend Cassio!

CASSIO   What make you from home?
        How is it with you, my most fair Bianca? 160
        I' faith, sweet love, I was coming to your house.

BIANCA   And I was going to your lodging, Cassio.
        What, keep a week away? Seven days, and nights?
        Eight score eight hours? And lovers' absent hours
        More tedious than the dial, eight score times! 165
        Oh weary reck'ning!

CASSIO   Pardon me, Bianca.
        I have this while with leaden thoughts been pressed;
        But I shall in a more continuate time
        Strike off this score of absence. Sweet Bianca,
        Take me this work out.

                      [*Gives her Desdemona's handkerchief*

BIANCA   Oh Cassio, whence came this? 170
        This is some token from a newer friend.
        To the felt absence now I feel a cause.
        Is 't come to this? Well, well.

CASSIO   Go to, woman!
        Throw your vile guesses in the devil's teeth
        From whence you have them. You are jealous now 175
        That this is from some mistress, some remembrance.
        No, by my faith, Bianca.

BIANCA   Why, whose is it?

CASSIO   I know not, neither. I found it in my chamber
        I like the work well; ere it be demanded,
        As like enough it will, I would have it copied. 180
        Take it and do't, and leave me for this time.

BIANCA   Leave you? Wherefore?

CASSIO   I do attend here on the General,
        And think it no addition, nor my wish,
        To have him see me womaned.

BIANCA   Why, I pray you? 185

CASSIO   Not that I love you not.

BIANCA   But that you do not love me!

187   *bring*   come with

191   *circumstanced*   put up with

> Compare Desdemona's pleas for Cassio's reinstatement in this scene with those that she made in Act 3 Scene 1. What do you think are the differences?

We see the first breakdown in communication between Othello and Desdemona in this scene and it is observed by Emilia. She could clear up the question of the missing handkerchief but she does not. Cassio again puts pressure on Desdemona to support him although every plea she makes further confirms to Othello that she has been unfaithful to him.

I pray you, bring me on the way a little,
And say if I shall see you soon at night.

CASSIO   'Tis but a little way that I can bring you,
For I attend here; but I'll see you soon.   **190**

BIANCA   'Tis very good; I must be circumstanced.

[*Exeunt*

4:1

Iago works on Othello's imagination creating pictures of Desdemona in bed with Cassio. Othello collapses in a fit. Iago engineers a situation where Othello can hear Cassio apparently speaking about Desdemona. What Othello does not know, though, is that Cassio is really talking about Bianca. Othello thinks he has conclusive proof of Desdemona's guilt when Bianca arrives clutching Desdemona's handkerchief.

2 *unauthorised* illicit

6 *hypocrisy against the devil* pretending to be more wicked than they are

7 *and yet do so* i.e. to be naked in bed together

Othello and Iago enter together in the middle of a conversation. What effect does this create? How can Iago's dominance be shown here? These exchanges show Othello following Iago's lead. How?

9 *a venial slip* a trivial sin

14 *honour* chastity

16 *essence* inner reality

17 *They have it very oft that have it not* those who seem to have honour often do not

21 *raven* a bird of ill-omen signifying death

22 *Boding* foretelling

25–9 *as knaves … must blab* they are villains who, once they have seduced a woman, either through their own pleading or her weakness, must tell everyone about it

31 *unswear* deny it

4:1   *Enter* OTHELLO *and* IAGO

IAGO	Will you think so?
OTHELLO	Think so, Iago?
IAGO	What,
	To kiss in private?
OTHELLO	An unauthorised kiss!
IAGO	Or to be naked with her friend in bed
	An hour or more, not meaning any harm?

OTHELLO   Naked in bed, Iago, and not mean harm?   5
It is hypocrisy against the devil.
They that mean virtuously and yet do so,
The devil their virtue tempts, and they tempt heaven.

IAGO   If they do nothing, 'tis a venial slip.
But if I give my wife a handkerchief –   10

OTHELLO   What then?

IAGO   Why then, 'tis hers, my lord; and being hers,
She may, I think, bestow 't on any man.

OTHELLO   She is protectress of her honour too.
May she give that?   15

IAGO   Her honour is an essence that's not seen;
They have it very oft that have it not.
But for the handkerchief –

OTHELLO   By heaven, I would most gladly have forgot it!
Thou saidst – oh, it comes o'er my memory   20
As doth the raven o'er the infected house,
Boding to all – he had my handkerchief.

IAGO   Ay, what of that?

OTHELLO   That's not so good now.

IAGO   What if I had said I had seen him do you wrong?
Or heard him say – as knaves be such abroad   25
Who having by their own importunate suit
Or voluntary dotage of some mistress
Convincèd or supplied them, cannot choose
But they must blab –

OTHELLO   Hath he said anything?

IAGO   He hath, my lord; but be you well assured,   30
No more than he'll unswear.

OTHELLO   What hath he said?

IAGO   Faith, that he did – I know not what he did.

OTHELLO   What? What?

IAGO   Lie.

36   *belie her* tell lies about her

37   *Zounds* by God's wounds (a strong oath)
       fulsome disgusting

39–40   *Nature would not … some instruction* no one could be put in
       such a rage without some cause

41   *Pish!* a strong, emotional exclamation

---

*As Othello breaks down completely, he speaks in prose rather than the poetic
blank verse that was associated with his character earlier. What effect is created
by these lines? What kind of voice would Othello use here? How would he move
about the stage? What expression might be on his face? Would he rant and
shout? Would he sound incredulous? Would he weep, perhaps fall to his knees,
stare into space? Which words would you particularly stress or emphasise?*

---

44   *medicine* poison
       credulous gullible

46   *reproach* shame

---

*How might Iago speak lines 43–7? Is he gloating? Or does he show concern?
Does he feel sympathy for the man he is destroying? In the 1985 RSC
production, David Suchet, as Iago, cradled Othello in his arms showing a
mixture of love and hate. Think of other ways this could be played.*

---

49   *epilepsy* fit

51   *forbear* leave him alone

52   *lethargy* unconsciousness
       have his quiet course run its natural course

56   *straight* soon

57   *great occasion* an important matter

60   *Would* I wish
       fortune situation

61   *hornèd* a cuckold

63   *civil* civilised

65–6   *Think every … with you* remember that every married man is in
       the same situation

67   *unproper beds* beds in which their wives are unfaithful

68   *Which they dare wear peculiar* which they think are theirs
       exclusively
       case situation

69   *fiend's arch-mock* the devil's greatest mockery

OTHELLO	With her?	
IAGO	With her, on her, what you will.	35
OTHELLO	Lie with her? Lie on her? – We say 'lie on her' when they belie her. – Lie with her! Zounds, that's fulsome! Handkerchief – confessions – handkerchief! To confess, and be hanged for his labour. First to be hanged, and then to confess! I tremble at it. Nature would not invest herself in such shadowing passion without some instruction. It is not words that shakes me thus. Pish! Noses, ears, and lips! Is 't possible – Confess? – Handkerchief? – Oh devil!	40

[*Falls in a trance*

IAGO	Work on!	
	My medicine works. Thus credulous fools are caught,	
	And many worthy and chaste dames even thus,	45
	All guiltless, meet reproach. What, ho! My lord!	
	My lord, I say! Othello!	

Enter CASSIO

How now, Cassio!

CASSIO	What's the matter?	
IAGO	My lord is fall'n into an epilepsy.	
	This is his second fit; he had one yesterday.	50
CASSIO	Rub him about the temples.	
IAGO	No, forbear.	
	The lethargy must have his quiet course.	
	If not, he foams at mouth, and by and by	
	Breaks out to savage madness. Look, he stirs.	
	Do you withdraw yourself a little while;	55
	He will recover straight. When he is gone,	
	I would on great occasion speak with you.	

[*Exit* CASSIO

	How is it, General? Have you not hurt your head?	
OTHELLO	Dost thou mock me?	
IAGO	I mock you not, by heaven.	
	Would you would bear your fortune like a man!	60
OTHELLO	A hornèd man's a monster and a beast.	
IAGO	There's many a beast then in a populous city,	
	And many a civil monster.	
OTHELLO	Did he confess it?	
IAGO	Good sir, be a man.	
	Think every bearded fellow that's but yoked	65
	May draw with you. There's millions now alive	
	That nightly lie in those unproper beds	
	Which they dare swear peculiar. Your case is better.	
	Oh, 'tis the spite of hell, the fiend's arch-mock,	

70   *lip* kiss
     wanton an adulterous woman
     secure couch free from suspicion in their marriage bed

71   *suppose her chaste* presume her innocent
     No, let me know I'd rather know

72   *I know what she shall be* I'd know she's a whore

74   *Confine ... list* keep control of yourself

77   *shifted him away* manage to get rid of him

78   *laid good 'scuses* give plausible explanations for
     ecstasy fit

80   *encave* hide

81   *fleers* sneers
     notable scorns obvious mockery

85   *cope* have sex with

86   *Marry* by the Virgin Mary (an oath)

87   *all in spleen* do everything out of rage

Notice Iago's repetition of 'man' (lines 60, 64, 76 and 88). What tone might he use to speak these lines? Is he comforting? Encouraging? Down-to-earth and practical? What is his purpose here?

91   *keep time* bide your time

93–4 *A housewife ... cloth* a prostitute that sells her body to buy
      herself food and clothing

95   *strumpet's plague* curse of the prostitute

96   *To beguile many and be beguiled by one* to deceive many men
     and be deceived by one

100 *unbookish* ignorant
     construe interpret

101 *light* light-hearted

103 *addition* title

104 *Whose want* the lack of which

105 *Ply* work on
     you are sure on 't i.e. sure of getting your title of Lieutenant back

107 *speed* succeed
     caitiff wretch

	To lip a wanton in a secure couch,	70
	And to suppose her chaste! No, let me know;	
	And knowing what I am, I know what she shall be.	
OTHELLO	Oh, thou art wise! 'Tis certain.	
IAGO	Stand you awhile apart;	

Confine yourself but in a patient list.
Whilst you were here, o'erwhelmèd with your grief – 75
A passion most unsuiting such a man –
Cassio came hither. I shifted him away
And laid good 'scuses upon your ecstasy;
Bade him anon return and here speak with me,
The which he promised. Do but encave yourself, 80
And mark the fleers, the gibes, and notable scorns
That dwell in every region of his face.
For I will make him tell the tale anew:
Where, how, how oft, how long ago, and when
He hath, and is again to cope your wife. 85
I say, but mark his gesture. Marry, patience!
Or I shall say you're all in all in spleen
And nothing of a man.

OTHELLO   Dost thou hear, Iago?
I will be found most cunning in my patience,
But – dost thou hear? – most bloody.

IAGO   That's not amiss, 90
But yet keep time in all. Will you withdraw?

                [OTHELLO *conceals himself at a distance*

Now will I question Cassio of Bianca,
A housewife that by selling her desires
Buys herself bread and cloth. It is a creature
That dotes on Cassio – as 'tis the strumpet's plague 95
To beguile many and be beguiled by one.
He, when he hears of her, cannot restrain
From the excess of laughter. Here he comes.

                Enter CASSIO

As he shall smile, Othello shall go mad;
And his unbookish jealousy must construe 100
Poor Cassio's smiles, gestures, and light behaviours
Quite in the wrong. How do you, Lieutenant?

CASSIO The worser that you give me the addition
Whose want even kills me.

IAGO   Ply Desdemona well, and you are sure on 't. 105
Now if this suit lay in Bianca's power,
How quickly should you speed!

CASSIO   Alas, poor caitiff!

OTHELLO   [*Aside*] Look how he laughs already!

135

111   *faintly* without much conviction
112   *importunes* begs
113   *Well said* well done
114   *gives it out* tells everyone
117   *triumph* gloat
      Roman i.e. like a Roman conqueror after a victory
118   *customer* prostitute
      bear some charity to my wit credit me with some sense
119   *unwholesome* corrupt
120   *They laugh that win* it will be my turn to laugh later
121   *cry* rumour
124   *scored* marked me down (as a cuckold)
130   *bauble* cheap plaything (i.e. Bianca)
      falls me thus about my neck throws her arm around my neck
131   *His gesture imports it* his action indicates it
137   *Before me!* Before god (an oath)

> To be successful, this part of the scene relies on the audience being convinced of the situation that Iago has engineered. If you were producing the play, how would you handle this section? Where would Othello stand so that he could see but not be seen? What tone would Cassio use? Is he disrespectful, flippant, mocking, joking, confidential, bragging? What gestures should he use? Does he put his arm around Iago as if talking to him man to man? Does he hang on Iago's neck mimicking Bianca's behaviour?

138   *such another* just like the other
      fitchew polecat (noted for being smelly)
142   *take out the work* copy the embroidery
      A likely piece of work a likely story

IAGO	I never knew woman love man so.	
CASSIO	Alas, poor rogue! I think, i' faith, she loves me.	110
OTHELLO	[*Aside*] Now he denies it faintly, and laughs it out.	
IAGO	Do you hear, Cassio?	

OTHELLO [*Aside*]   Now he importunes him
    To tell it o'er. Go to! Well said, well said!

IAGO   She gives it out that you shall marry her.
    Do you intend it?   115

CASSIO   Ha, ha, ha!

OTHELLO [*Aside*] Do you triumph, Roman? Do you triumph?

CASSIO   I marry – what? A customer? Prithee bear some charity to my wit;
    do not think it so unwholesome. Ha, ha, ha!

OTHELLO [*Aside*] So, so, so, so! They laugh that win.   120

IAGO   Faith, the cry goes that you marry her.

CASSIO   Prithee, say true.

IAGO   I am a very villain else.

OTHELLO [*Aside*] Have you scored me? Well.

CASSIO   This is the monkey's own giving out. She is persuaded I will marry   125
    her out of her own love and flattery, not out of my promise.

OTHELLO [*Aside*] Iago beckons me: now he begins the story.
                                        [*He moves close enough to hear*

CASSIO   She was here even now; she haunts me in every place. I was the
    other day talking on the sea bank with certain Venetians, and thither
    comes the bauble, and falls me thus about my neck –   130

OTHELLO [*Aside*] Crying, 'Oh, dear Cassio!' as it were. His gesture imports it.

CASSIO   So hangs, and lolls, and weeps upon me; so shakes and pulls me!
    Ha, ha, ha!

OTHELLO [*Aside*] Now he tells how she plucked him to my chamber. Oh, I see
    that nose of yours, but not that dog I shall throw it to.   135

CASSIO   Well, I must leave her company.

IAGO   Before me! look where she comes.

                        Enter BIANCA

CASSIO   'Tis such another fitchew! – Marry, a perfumed one! What do you
    mean by this haunting of me?

BIANCA   Let the devil and his dam haunt you! What did you mean by that   140
    same handkerchief you gave me even now? I was a fine fool to take it.
    I must take out the work? A likely piece of work that you should find it
    in your chamber and know not who left it there! This is some minx's
    token, and I must take out the work?
    There! [*Gives* CASSIO *the handkerchief*]   145

146   *hobby-horse* whore

> *What dramatic effect is achieved by the entry of Bianca? What tone could Othello use to speak the line* **By heaven, that should be my handkerchief!***? Does he sound angry? Menacing? Amazed? Sad? Shocked?*

151   *when you are next prepared for* when I'm ready for you

153   *rail* make a fuss
else otherwise

156   *fain* much like to

164   *prizes* values

166   *I would … nine years a-killing* I would to spend nine years killing him slowly

173   *that's not your way* that's not the right way to go

176   *wit and invention* intelligence and imagination

178–9   *of so gentle a condition* so yielding in character

180   *Ay, too gentle* i.e. yes, she gives in too easily

183   *fond over her iniquity* indulgent of her sinfulness
patent licence

184   *touch* affect
comes near concerns

185   *messes* pieces of meat

> *Look at lines 159–96. Here we see the conflict within Othello between his love for Desdemona and his jealous fury at her supposed infidelity. Which lines stress this conflict? How could this conflict be emphasised through the way that Othello speaks these lines? Does he speak with anger, bitterness, regret, or does he fluctuate between anger or bitterness and a softer, regretful or loving tone?*

Give it your hobby-horse, wheresoever you had it. I'll take out no work on 't.

CASSIO   How now, my sweet Bianca! How now, how now!

OTHELLO [*Aside*] By heaven, that should be my handkerchief!

BIANCA   If you'll come to supper tonight, you may; if you will not, come   150
when you are next prepared for.   [*Exit*

IAGO   After her, after her!

CASSIO   Faith, I must; she'll rail in the streets else.

IAGO   Will you sup there?

CASSIO   Faith, I intend so.   155

IAGO   Well, I may chance to see you, for I would very fain speak with you.

CASSIO   Prithee come, will you?

IAGO   Go to, say no more.   [*Exit* CASSIO

OTHELLO [*Coming forward*] How shall I murder him, Iago?

IAGO   Did you perceive how he laughed at his vice?   160

OTHELLO   Oh, Iago!

IAGO   And did you see the handkerchief?

OTHELLO   Was that mine?

IAGO   Yours, by this hand! And to see how he prizes the foolish woman
your wife! She gave it him, and he hath given it his whore.   165

OTHELLO   I would have him nine years a-killing! –
A fine woman, a fair woman, a sweet woman!

IAGO   Nay, you must forget that.

OTHELLO   Ay, let her rot, and perish, and be damned tonight, for she shall not
live. No, my heart is turned to stone: I strike it, and it hurts my hand. –   170
Oh, the world hath not a sweeter creature! She might lie by an
emperor's side and command him tasks.

IAGO   Nay, that's not your way.

OTHELLO   Hang her! – I do but say what she is: so delicate with her needle; an
admirable musician. Oh, she will sing the savageness out of a bear! Of   175
so high and plenteous wit and invention!

IAGO   She's the worse for all this.

OTHELLO   Oh, a thousand, a thousand times. – And then, of so gentle a
condition!

IAGO   Ay, too gentle.   180

OTHELLO   Nay, that's certain. – But yet the pity of it, Iago! Oh Iago, the pity of
it, Iago!

IAGO   If you are so fond over her iniquity, give her patent to offend; for if
it touch not you, it comes near nobody.

OTHELLO   I will chop her into messes! Cuckold me!   185

189 *expostulate with her* discuss things with her

190 *unprovide my mind* weaken my determination

194 *let me be his undertaker* let me kill him

201 *the instrument of their pleasures* the letter from the Duke and the Senate giving their command

208 *unkind breach* a breakdown of relationship

215 *atone them* reconcile them

216 *Fire and brimstone* hell (an oath)

IAGO	Oh, 'tis foul in her.
OTHELLO	With mine officer!
IAGO	That's fouler.
OTHELLO	Get me some poison, Iago, this night. I'll not expostulate with her, lest her body and beauty unprovide my mind again. This night, Iago! 190
IAGO	Do it not with poison. Strangle her in her bed, even the bed she hath contaminated.
OTHELLO	Good. Good. The justice of it pleases. Very good.
IAGO	And for Cassio, let me be his undertaker. You shall hear more by midnight. 195
OTHELLO	Excellent, good!

Trumpet sounds

What trumpet is that same?

IAGO	I warrant, something from Venice.

Enter **LODOVICO**, **DESDEMONA** *and* **ATTENDANTS**

'Tis Lodovico.
This comes from the Duke. See, your wife's with him.

LODOVICO	God save you, worthy General!
OTHELLO	With all my heart, sir!
LODOVICO	The Duke and senators of Venice greet you. [*Gives* **OTHELLO** *a letter* 200
OTHELLO	I kiss the instrument of their pleasures. [*Reads the letter*
DESDEMONA	And what's the news; good cousin Lodovico?
IAGO	I am very glad to see you, signor. Welcome to Cyprus.
LODOVICO	I thank you. How does Lieutenant Cassio? 205
IAGO	Lives, sir.
DESDEMONA	Cousin, there's fall'n between him and my lord An unkind breach, but you shall make all well.
OTHELLO	Are you sure of that?
DESDEMONA	My lord? 210
OTHELLO [*Reads*]	'This fail you not to do, as you will –'
LODOVICO	He did not call; he's busy in the paper. Is there division 'twixt my lord and Cassio?
DESDEMONA	A most unhappy one. I would do much To atone them, for the love I bear to Cassio. 215
OTHELLO	Fire and brimstone!
DESDEMONA	My lord?
OTHELLO	Are you wise?
DESDEMONA	What, is he angry?

219	*Deputing Cassio in his government* appointing Cassio to replace him as Governor
221	*mad* mad with pleasure at Cassio's promotion
225	*'Tis very much* this is terrible
228	*prove a crocodile* Crocodiles were supposed to shed false tears to lure victims – this relates to Othello's view that Desdemona's tears are false.
235–7	*turn, and turn … and turn again* The initial reference is to bringing her back but here there is an implication of her being fickle.
238	*obedient* she will do whatever you say (again with a sexual connotation)
240	*well painted* well imitated
243	*avaunt* go
246	*Goats and monkeys!* a cry of rage (again with sexual connotations)

> *What effect is created by Othello's speech (lines 235–46)? In the BBC Shakespeare production Othello (Anthony Hopkins) angrily drags Desdemona, turning her round and round, and as she leaves pulls a grotesques face at her while making a gutteral, animal-like sound. As he speaks to Lodovico, his speech is more controlled although there is a barely suppressed rage evident in his manner. As he looks at the mandate ordering him to return to Venice, he tears it up when he repeats the part where it says that Cassio is to replace him. How would he speak the final line:* **Goats and monkeys!**? *In the BBC production, he speaks this line with real venom and spits as he leaves. What image is suggested to the audience from this phrase?*

248	*all in all sufficient* completely reliable
249–51	*Whose solid … nor pierce* whose solid goodness could not be wounded or killed by poison

LODOVICO   May be the letter moved him;
 For, as I think, they do command him home,
 Deputing Cassio in his government.

DESDEMONA By my troth, I am glad on 't.

OTHELLO   Indeed?

DESDEMONA   My lord?   **220**

OTHELLO   I am glad to see you mad.

DESDEMONA   Why, sweet Othello –

OTHELLO   Devil!   [*Strikes her*

DESDEMONA I have not deserved this.

LODOVICO   My lord, this would not be believed in Venice
 Though I should swear I saw 't. 'Tis very much.   **225**
 Make her amends; she weeps.

OTHELLO   Oh devil, devil!
 If that the earth could teem with woman's tears,
 Each drop she falls would prove a crocodile.
 Out of my sight!

DESDEMONA [*Going*] I will not stay to offend you.   **230**

LODOVICO   Truly, an obedient lady.
 I do beseech your lordship, call her back.

OTHELLO   Mistress!

DESDEMONA   My lord?   [*Returning*

OTHELLO   What would you with her, sir?

LODOVICO   Who? I, my lord?

OTHELLO   Ay! You did wish that I would make her turn.   **235**
 Sir, she can turn, and turn, and yet go on,
 And turn again; and she can weep, sir, weep;
 And she's obedient; as you say, obedient,
 Very obedient. Proceed you in your tears.
 Concerning this, sir – oh, well-painted passion! –   **240**
 I am commanded home. – Get you away,
 I'll send for you anon. – Sir, I obey the mandate
 And will return to Venice. – Hence, avaunt!

            [*Exit* DESDEMONA

 Cassio shall have my place. And, sir, tonight
 I do entreat that we may sup together.   **245**
 You are welcome, sir, to Cyprus. – Goats and monkeys!   [*Exit*

LODOVICO   Is this the noble Moor whom our full senate
 Call all in all sufficient? Is this the nature
 Whom passion could not shake? Whose solid virtue
 The shot of accident nor dart of chance   **250**
 Could neither graze nor pierce?

252	*Are his wits safe?* Is he sane?
253	*censure* judgement
254–5	*What he … he were* Othello isn't himself – I wish he were
257	*use* unusual behaviour
258	*work upon his blood* make him angry
259	*new create his fault* make him behave like this for the first time
262	*courses will denote* actions will reveal

Compare the methods that Iago uses in this scene to increase Othello's jealousy with those that he used in Act 3 Scene 3.

Iago works on Othello's imagination, suggesting to him pictures of Desdemona in bed with Cassio. Othello collapses in a fit, overcome with jealousy and, when he recovers, Iago makes sure that he is in a position to see Cassio apparently laughing and mocking. Othello thinks he is laughing about Desdemona's sexual advances to him. Bianca arrives with the handkerchief and Othello takes this as the final proof of his wife's guilt. He plans to kill her while Iago kills Cassio.

4:2

Othello questions Emilia about Desdemona and Cassio. Emilia is ordered to bring Desdemona to Othello and he accuses her of being unfaithful to him. She protests her innocence but cannot convince him that she is true to him. He furiously calls her a whore and leaves her. She is completely baffled and upset by his behaviour and she turns to Iago for help. He reassures her, telling her that it is just the mood he is in.

| 5 | *made up* spoken |

IAGO   He is much changed.

LODOVICO   Are his wits safe? Is he not light of brain?

IAGO   He's that he is; I may not breathe my censure.
         What he might be – if what he might he is not –
         I would to heaven he were!

LODOVICO   What, strike his wife?   **255**

IAGO   Faith, that was not so well; yet would I knew
         That stroke would prove the worst.

LODOVICO   Is it his use?
         Or did the letters work upon his blood
         And new create his fault?

IAGO   Alas, alas!
         It is not honesty in me to speak   **260**
         What I have seen and known. You shall observe him,
         And his own courses will denote him so,
         That I may save my speech. Do but go after
         And mark how he continues.

LODOVICO   I am sorry that I am deceived in him.   **265**

                                                    [*Exeunt*

4:2   *Enter* OTHELLO *and* EMILIA

OTHELLO   You have seen nothing, then?

EMILIA   Nor ever heard, nor ever did suspect.

OTHELLO   Yes, you have seen Cassio and she together.

EMILIA   But then I saw no harm, and then I heard
         Each syllable that breath made up between them.   5

OTHELLO   What, did they never whisper?

EMILIA   Never, my lord.

OTHELLO   Nor send you out o' the way?

EMILIA   Never.

OTHELLO   To fetch her fan, her gloves, her mask, nor nothing?

EMILIA   Never, my lord.

11   *durst* dare

12   *Lay down my soul at stake* I'd bet my life

13   *abuse your bosom* deceive you

15   *requite* punish
     serpent's curse God's curse on Satan

17   *happy* content (that his wife is faithful)

19   *She says enough* she says what you'd expect her to say

> The scene begins with Othello questioning Emilia about Desdemona. What attitude does she show towards Othello? Does she treat him with respect, incredulity or does she find it hard to conceal the contempt that she feels for him because of what he has done to Desdemona? What effect is created by her repetition of 'never'? How might she speak this word?

19–20   *she's a simple ... as much* even a simple-minded brothel keeper could say what she has said

20   *subtle* cunning

21   *A closet ... villainous secrets* someone who keeps her wicked activities hidden away

23   *chuck* a term of affection

25   *horrible fancy* strange fantasy

26   *Some of your function* do your job (i.e. as a brothel keeper)

27   *procreants* people who are having sex

28   *cry 'hem'* give a warning by clearing your throat

29   *mystery* trade
     dispatch hurry up

> What do Desdemona's short questions indicate here? Fear? Apprehension? Bewilderment? How might her tone indicate her feelings? Does her voice tremble or is she on control of her emotions?

30   *import* mean

35   *like one of heaven* like an angel

41   *heavy* unhappy

42   *motive* cause

43   *haply* perhaps

OTHELLO	That's strange.	10

EMILIA   I durst, my lord, to wager she is honest,
Lay down my soul at stake. If you think other,
Remove your thought: it doth abuse your bosom.
If any wretch have put this in your head,
Let heaven requite it with the serpent's curse!   15
For if she be not honest, chaste, and true,
There's no man happy – the purest of their wives
Is foul as slander.

OTHELLO   Bid her come hither. Go!   [*Exit* EMILIA
She says enough; yet she's a simple bawd
That cannot say as much. This is a subtle whore,   20
A closet lock and key of villainous secrets,
And yet she'll kneel and pray; I have seen her do't.

Enter DESDEMONA *and* EMILIA

DESDEMONA My lord, what is your will?

OTHELLO   Pray you, chuck, come hither.

DESDEMONA What is your pleasure?

OTHELLO   Let me see your eyes.
Look in my face.

DESDEMONA   What horrible fancy's this?   25

OTHELLO [*To* EMILIA] Some of your function, mistress:
Leave procreants alone and shut the door;
Cough or cry 'hem' if anybody come.
Your mystery, your mystery! Nay, dispatch!   [*Exit* EMILIA

DESDEMONA Upon my knee, what doth your speech import?   30
I understand a fury in your words,
But not the words.

OTHELLO   Why, what art thou?

DESDEMONA Your wife, my lord; your true and loyal wife.

OTHELLO   Come, swear it; damn thyself,
Lest being like one of heaven, the devils themselves   35
Should fear to seize thee. Therefore be double-damned:
Swear thou art honest.

DESDEMONA   Heaven doth truly know it.

OTHELLO   Heaven truly knows that thou art false as hell.

DESDEMONA To whom, my lord? With whom? How am I false?

OTHELLO   Ah, Desdemona! Away! Away! Away!   40

DESDEMONA Alas the heavy day! Why do you weep?
Am I the motive of these tears, my lord?
If haply you my father do suspect

44	*An instrument of* being the cause of *your calling back* being called back to Venice
45	*lost him* offended him (lost his love)
47	*try me* test me
49	*Steeped* soaked
53–4	*The fixed … moving finger* a permanent figure of ridicule
56	*there* i.e. Desdemona *garnered up my heart* stored up all my emotions
58	*fountain* source
61	*knot and gender* intertwine together and breed *Turn thy complexion there* turn pale
62	*cherubin* angel

> In some productions, Othello's speech (lines 46–63) is spoken directly to Desdemona, sometimes with Othello gripping her shoulders or pulling her to him or squeezing her cheeks with his hand. Other productions have him delivering this speech almost as a soliloquy. What are your ideas on the most effective way this could be delivered? Should the audience feel sympathy at this point for Othello or for Desdemona?

64	*honest* chaste
65	*shambles* slaughter-house
66	*quicken even with the blowing* come to life the moment they are laid as eggs
69	*ignorant* unintentional
70	*fair paper … goodly book* i.e. Desdemona herself
72	*commoner* prostitute
73	*make very forges of my cheeks* cheeks to redden as fiercely as a blacksmith's forge
74	*That would … modesty* that would burn up all sense of shame
76	*stops* closes up *the moon* a symbol of chastity *winks* turns a blind eye
77	*bawdy wind … all it meets* the wind is like a whore because it kisses everyone it comes into contact with
78	*mine* cave
81	*strumpet* whore
82	*this vessel* my body

An instrument of this your calling back,
Lay not your blame on me. If you have lost him, 45
I have lost him too.

OTHELLO   Had it pleased heaven
To try me with affliction, had they rained
All kind of sores and shames on my bare head,
Steeped me in poverty to the very lips,
Given to captivity me and my utmost hopes, 50
I should have found in some place of my soul
A drop of patience. But alas, to make me
The fixèd figure for the time of scorn
To point his slow and moving finger at –
Yet could I bear that too, well, very well; 55
But there where I have garnered up my heart,
Where either I must live or bear no life,
The fountain from the which my current runs
Or else dries up – to be discarded thence,
Or keep it as a cistern for foul toads 60
To knot and gender in! Turn thy complexion there,
Patience, thou young and rose-lipped cherubin!
I here look grim as hell.

DESDEMONA I hope my noble lord esteems me honest.

OTHELLO   Oh ay; as summer flies are in the shambles, 65
That quicken even with blowing. Oh thou weed,
Who art so lovely fair, and smell'st so sweet,
That the sense aches at thee, would thou hadst never been born!

DESDEMONA Alas, what ignorant sin have I committed?

OTHELLO   Was this fair paper, this most goodly book, 70
Made to write 'whore' upon? What committed?
Committed? Oh thou public commoner!
I should make very forges of my cheeks,
That would to cinders burn up modesty,
Did I but speak thy deeds. What committed? 75
Heaven stops the nose at it, and the moon winks;
The bawdy wind, that kisses all it meets,
Is hushed within the hollow mine of earth
And will not hear 't. What committed?

DESDEMONA By heaven, you do me wrong. 80

OTHELLO   Are not you a strumpet?

DESDEMONA   No, as I am a Christian.
If to preserve this vessel for my lord
From any other, foul, unlawful touch
Be not to be a strumpet, I am none.

OTHELLO   What, not a whore?

149

87	*cry you mercy* beg your pardon
90	*office* job
	Saint Peter keeps the gates of heaven
92	*done our course* finished our business
93	*keep our counsel* keep our business private
94	*conceive* imagine

Faith, half asleep *seems an unusual thing for Desdemona to say at this point. What do you think she means? How might she say this? Wearily? Bewildered? Like someone suffering emotional exhaustion? Like someone who doesn't believe or understand what is happening?*

96	*half asleep* dazed (by Othello's attack)
102	*go by water* expressed through tears
105	*meet* fitting
106–7	*stick … misuse* have the slightest reason to criticise my smallest fault
111	*chid* told me off
112	*I am a child to chiding* I'm not used to being told off
113	*bewhored* called her a whore
114	*despite* abuse
	heavy terms violent words

DESDEMONA	No, as I shall be saved!	**85**
OTHELLO	Is 't possible?	
DESDEMONA	Oh, heaven forgive us!	

OTHELLO   I cry you mercy then.
I took you for that cunning whore of Venice
That married with Othello. [*Calling*] You, mistress,
That have the office opposite to Saint Peter   **90**
And keeps the gate of hell!

Enter EMILIA

                              You, you, ay, you!
We have done our course: there's money for your pains.
I pray you turn the key, and keep our counsel.   [*Exit*

EMILIA   Alas, what does this gentleman conceive?
How do you, madam? How do you, my good lady?   **95**

DESDEMONA Faith, half asleep.

EMILIA   Good madam, what's the matter with my lord?

DESDEMONA With who?

EMILIA   Why, with my lord, madam.

DESDEMONA Who is thy lord?

EMILIA   He that is yours, sweet lady.

DESDEMONA I have none. Do not talk to me, Emilia;   **100**
I cannot weep, nor answers have I none
But what should go by water. Prithee, tonight
Lay on my bed my wedding sheets, remember,
And call thy husband hither.

EMILIA   Here's a change indeed!   [*Exit*

DESDEMONA 'Tis meet I should be used so, very meet.   **105**
How have I been behaved, that he might stick
The small'st opinion on my least misuse?

Enter IAGO *and* EMILIA

IAGO   What is your pleasure, madam? How is 't with you?

DESDEMONA I cannot tell. Those that do teach young babes
Do it with gentle means and easy tasks;   **110**
He might have chid me so, for in good faith
I am a child to chiding.

IAGO   What is the matter, lady?

EMILIA   Alas, Iago, my lord hath so bewhored her,
Thrown such despite and heavy terms upon her,
That true hearts cannot hear it.   **115**

DESDEMONA Am I that name, Iago?

IAGO   What name, fair lady?

119   *callet*   slut

123   *forsook*   given up

126   *Beshrew*   curse

127   *trick*   delusion

129   *busy*   interfering
       insinuating   wheedling to gain favour

130   *cogging*   deceiving
       cozening   cheating
       to get some office   to get promoted

> *What is the irony of these lines? How could the actors speak these lines? Could there be any humour here? Does Iago act as if genuinely concerned or does he give a fleeting smirk towards the audience as he says* **Fie, there is no such man!?**

134   *halter pardon him*   may he hang (i.e. the halter is a noose)

137   *abused*   misled

138   *base notorious*   low reputation

139   *Oh heaven … unfold*   I wish that heaven would expose such villains

142   *within door*   quietly

143   *squire*   young fellow

144   *the seamy side without*   inside out

146   *go to*   be quiet

> *Iago wants Emilia to keep quiet here. Why? How does he try to keep control of the situation?*

148   *this light of heaven*   the moon, i.e. the symbol of chastity

151   *discourse of thought*   thought processes

DESDEMONA Such as she said my lord did say I was.

EMILIA He called her whore. A beggar in his drink
Could not have laid such terms upon his callet.

IAGO Why did he so?   **120**

DESDEMONA I do not know. I am sure I am none such.

IAGO Do not weep, do not weep. Alas the day!

EMILIA Hath she forsook so many noble matches,
Her father, and her country, and her friends,
To be called whore? Would it not make one weep?   **125**

DESDEMONA It is my wretched fortune.

IAGO   Beshrew him for it!
How comes this trick upon him?

DESDEMONA   Nay, heaven doth know.

EMILIA I will be hanged if some eternal villain,
Some busy and insinuating rogue,
Some cogging, cozening slave, to get some office,   **130**
Have not devised this slander; I will be hanged else.

IAGO Fie, there is no such man! It is impossible.

DESDEMONA If any such there be, heaven pardon him.

EMILIA A halter pardon him, and hell gnaw his bones!
Why should he call her whore? Who keeps her company?   **135**
What place, what time, what form, what likelihood?
The Moor's abused by some most villainous knave,
Some base notorious knave, some scurvy fellow.
Oh heaven, that such companions thou'dst unfold,
And put in every honest hand a whip   **140**
To lash the rascals naked through the world
Even from the east to the west!

IAGO   Speak within door.

EMILIA Oh fie upon them! Some such squire he was
That turned your wit the steamy side without
And made you to suspect me with the Moor.   **145**

IAGO You are a fool: go to.

DESDEMONA   Alas, Iago,
What shall I do to win my lord again?
Good friend, go to him; for by this light of heaven,
I know not how I lost him. Here I kneel:
If e'er my will did trespass 'gainst his love,   **150**
Either in discourse of thought or actual deed;
Or that mine eyes, mine ears, or any sense,
Delighted them in any other form;
Or that I do not yet, and ever did,
And ever will – though he do shake me off   **155**

157	*forswear* abandon
158	*defeat* destroy
160	*abhor* disgust
161–2	*To do … make me* I wouldn't do anything that would give me the title whore for anything in the world
163	*humour* mood
164	*does him offence* troubles him
165	*chide with you* takes it out on you
166	*warrant* promise
168	*stays the meat* wait for their meal
172	*What in the contrary* What makes you think I don't
173	*thou daff'st me* you put me off *device* ploy
174	*conveniency* opportunity
176	*put up in peace* put up with quietly
179–80	*your words and performances are no kin together* what you say and what you do are different things
182	*wasted myself out of my means* I have spent everything I have
184	*votarist* nun
185	*returned me* sent back to me *expectations and comforts* hopes and encouragements *of sudden respect* that she would immediately take notice of me
187	*Well, go to* OK, OK
189	*scurvy* shameful *fopped* cheated
192	*suit* request
193	*solicitation* wooing *seek satisfaction* i.e. either by getting his money and jewels back or by a duel

To beggarly divorcement – love him dearly;
Comfort forswear me! Unkindness may do much,
And his unkindness may defeat my life,
But never taint my love. I cannot say, 'whore' –
It does abhor me now I speak the word;   **160**
To do the act that might the addition earn
Not the world's mass of vanity could make me.

IAGO   I pray you be content: 'tis but his humour;
The business of the state does him offence,
And he does chide with you.   **165**

DESDEMONA If 'twere no other –

IAGO   It is but so, I warrant.

Trumpets sound

Hark how these instruments summon to supper.
The messengers of Venice stays the meat.
Go in, and weep not; all things shall be well.

[*Exeunt* DESDEMONA *and* EMILIA

Enter RODERIGO

How now, Roderigo?   **170**

RODERIGO   I do not find that thou deal'st justly with me.

IAGO   What in the contrary?

RODERIGO   Every day thou daff'st me with some device, Iago, and rather, as it
seems to me now, keeps't from me all conveniency, than suppliest me
with the least advantage of hope. I will indeed no longer endure it; nor   **175**
am I yet persuaded to put up in peace what already I have foolishly
suffered.

IAGO   Will you hear me, Roderigo?

RODERIGO   Faith, I have heard too much, and your words and performances are
no kin together.   **180**

IAGO   You charge me most unjustly.

RODERIGO   With naught but truth. I have wasted myself out of my means. The
jewels you have had from me to deliver Desdemona would half have
corrupted a votarist. You have told me she hath received them, and
returned me expectations and comforts of sudden respect and   **185**
acquaintance; but I find none.

IAGO   Well, go to; very well.

RODERIGO   Very well, go to? I cannot go to, man, nor 'tis not very well. Nay, I
think it is scurvy, and begin to find myself fopped in it.

IAGO   Very well.   **190**

RODERIGO   I tell you 'tis not very well. I will make myself known to Desdemona.
If she will return me my jewels, I will give over my suit and repent my
unlawful solicitation. If not, assure yourself I will seek satisfaction of you.

194   *You have said now*   you have committed yourself

195   *protest intendment of doing*   state the intention of doing

196   *mettle*   spirit

198   *taken … exception*   a reasonable complaint about my behaviour

199   *directly*   honestly

200   *It hath not appeared*   it doesn't look like it

202   *wit*   perception

205   *enjoy*   have sex with

206   *engines for my life*   plots to kill me

The first real threat to Iago occurs with the entry of Roderigo. How has Roderigo's attitude changed? How could this be shown in how he acts towards Iago? Which line really confirms his threat towards Iago? Does he threaten him physically? What kind of response does Iago show here? Is he genuinely surprised? Does he show fear or does he respond with anger himself? In one production, Iago draws his sword at this point and briefly threatens Roderigo in return, whereas in the 1995 film version Roderigo is presented as potentially a much more dangerous character whose threat to Iago is very real.

207   *within reason and compass*   sensible and practical

212   *Mauritania*   an area of North Africa

213   *abode be lingered here*   his stay here is lengthened

214   *determinate*   decisive

220   *harlotry*   whore

220–1   *his honourable fortune*   i.e. his promotion

222   *fashion to fall out*   arrange to happen

222–3   *take him at your pleasure*   attack him when you feel the moment is right

223   *second*   back up

224   *stand not amazed at it*   don't stand there bewildered

226–7   *grows to waste*   is passing

Compare Roderigo's attitude towards Iago in this scene with that seen in Acts 1 and 2. How does it differ? Why? Does Iago handle Roderigo here in just the same way as in previous acts or does he use a different technique?

Desdemona protests her innocence and shows the constancy of her love for Othello, but nothing she says convinces him and he leaves, calling her a whore. She tries to understand what is wrong and asks the advice of Iago. He appears to reassure her. Iago involves Roderigo in a plot to kill Cassio.

IAGO	You have said now.	
RODERIGO	Ay, and said nothing but what I protest intendment of doing.	195

IAGO   Why, now I see there's mettle in thee, and even from this instant do build on thee a better opinion than ever before. Give me thy hand, Roderigo. Thou hast taken against me a most just exception; but yet I protest I have dealt most directly in thy affair.

RODERIGO   It hath not appeared.   200

IAGO   I grant indeed it hath not appeared, and your suspicion is not without wit and judgement. But, Roderigo, if thou hast that in thee indeed, which I have greater reason to believe now than ever – I mean purpose, courage, and valour – this night show it. If thou the next night following enjoy not Desdemona, take me from this world with   205
treachery, and devise engines for my life.

RODERIGO   Well, what is it? Is it within reason and compass?

IAGO   Sir, there is especial commission come from Venice to depute Cassio in Othello's place.

RODERIGO   Is that true? Why, then Othello and Desdemona return again to   210
Venice.

IAGO   Oh, no; he goes into Mauritania and taketh away with him the fair Desdemona, unless his abode be lingered here by some accident; wherein none can be so determinate as the removing of Cassio.

RODERIGO   How do you mean removing him?   215

IAGO   Why, by making him uncapable of Othello's place – knocking out his brains.

RODERIGO   And that you would have me to do.

IAGO   Ay, if you dare do yourself a profit and a right. He sups tonight with a harlotry, and thither will I go to him. He knows not yet of his   220
honourable fortune. If you will watch his going thence – which I will fashion to fall out between twelve and one – you may take him at your pleasure. I will be near to second your attempt, and he shall fall between us. Come, stand not amazed at it, but go along with me. I will show you such a necessity in his death that you shall think yourself   225
bound to put it on him. It is now high supper time, and the night grows to waste. About it!

RODERIGO   I will hear further reason for this.

IAGO   And you shall be satisfied.

[Exeunt

4:3

Othello sends Desdemona to bed and tells her to dismiss Emilia. Alone, Emilia tells her that she has put the wedding sheets on the bed as she was asked. Desdemona asks Emilia to wrap her in one of the sheets if she dies. She sings a sad song about an unhappy love and talks to Emilia about faithfulness in marriage.

1   *beseech*   beg

7   *on the instant*   immediately
     forthwith   straightaway

8   *Look it be done*   make sure it's done

Does Othello's manner towards Lodovico contrast with the way he speaks to, and acts towards, Desdemona? In some productions, he speaks quietly and civilly to both Lodovico and Desdemona. In others, his voice is harsh and threatening when he speaks to Desdemona. How do you think these lines can be most effectively delivered?

11   *incontinent*   immediately

18   *So would not I*   I don't (i.e. wish I'd never seen him)
     approve   commend

19   *stubbornness*   rough behaviour
     checks   rebukes

22   *All's one*   it doesn't matter now

23   *shroud me*   prepare my body for burial

24   *You talk*   talk nonsense

27   *forsake*   desert
     Willow   the tree traditionally associated with weeping

30–1   *I have much … my head*   I'm finding it difficult not to hang my head

32   *dispatch*   hurry up

34   *proper man*   a handsome man

4:3   *Enter* **OTHELLO, LODOVICO, DESDEMONA, EMILIA,** *and* ATTENDANTS

LODOVICO   I do beseech you, sir, trouble yourself no further.

OTHELLO   Oh, pardon me; 't will do me good to walk.

LODOVICO   Madam, good night. I humbly thank your ladyship.

DESDEMONA   Your honour is most welcome.

OTHELLO   Will you walk, sir?
        Oh, Desdemona.   5

DESDEMONA   My lord?

OTHELLO   Get you to bed on the instant; I will be returned forthwith.
        Dismiss your attendant there. Look it be done.

DESDEMONA   I will, my lord.

                  [Exeunt **OTHELLO, LODOVICO,** *and* ATTENDANTS

EMILIA   How goes it now? He looks gentler than he did.   10

DESDEMONA   He says he will return incontinent,
        And hath commanded me to go to bed,
        And bade me to dismiss you.

EMILIA   Dismiss me?

DESDEMONA   It was his bidding; therefore, good Emilia,
        Give me my nightly wearing, and adieu.   15
        We must not now displease him.

EMILIA   I would you had never seen him.

DESDEMONA   So would not I: my love doth so approve him
        That even his stubbornness, his checks, his frowns –
        Prithee unpin me – have grace and favour.   20

EMILIA   I have laid those sheets you bade me on the bed.

DESDEMONA   All's one. Good Father, how foolish are our minds!
        If I do die before thee, prithee shroud me
        In one of these same sheets.

EMILIA   Come, some! You talk.

DESDEMONA   My mother had a maid called Barbary.   25
        She was in love; and he she loved proved mad
        And did forsake her. She had a song of 'Willow';
        An old thing 'twas, but it expressed her fortune,
        And she died singing it. That song tonight
        Will not go from my mind; I have much to do   30
        But to go hang my head all at one side,
        And sing it like poor Barbary – prithee dispatch.

EMILIA   Shall I go fetch your nightgown?

DESDEMONA   No, unpin me here.
        This Lodovico is a proper man.

37   *nether* lower

45   *Lay by these* put these away

47   *hie thee* hurry
      anon soon

49   *his scorn I approve* I accept his scorn

> *Desdemona's mood has changed from that of the previous scene. How might this be reflected in her tone of voice? Is she sad? Wistful? Resigned? Or does she try to carry on as if all is well?*

54   *couch* sleep with

56   *bode* foretell

58   *Dost thou in conscience think* do you really think

59   *abuse* deceive

60   *In such gross kind* in such a disgusting way

62   *this heavenly light* the moon

69   *undo't* undo it

70   *joint-ring* a ring made in two parts that fit together
      measures of lawn pieces of linen

71   *petty exhibition* small gift

EMILIA   A very handsome man.

DESMEMONA   He speaks well.   35

EMILIA   I know a lady in Venice would have walked barefoot to Palestine for
a touch of his nether lip.

DESDEMONA *sings*
The poor soul sat sighing by a sycamore tree,
   Sing all a green willow;
Her hand on her bosom, her head on her knee,   40
   Sing willow, willow, willow.
The fresh streams ran by her and murmured her moans;
   Sing willow, willow, willow.
Her salt tears fell from her and softened the stones –
[*Speaks*] Lay by these –   45
[*Sings*] Sing willow, willow, willow –
[*Speaks*] Prithee hie thee; he'll come anon.
[*Sings*] Sing all a green willow must be my garland.
Let nobody blame him; his scorn I approve –
[*Speaks*] Nay, that's not next. Hark, who is 't that knocks?   50

EMILIA   It is the wind.

DESDEMONA *sings*
I called my love false love, but what said he then?
   Sing willow, willow, willow.
'If I court more women, you'll couch with more men.'
[*Speaks*] So, get thee gone; good night. Mine eyes do itch.   55
Does that bode weeping?

EMILIA   'Tis neither here nor there.

DESDEMONA I have heard it said so. Oh, these men, these men!
Dost thou in conscience think – tell me, Emilia –
That there be women do abuse their husbands
In such gross kind?

EMILIA   There be some such, no question.   60

DESDEMONA Wouldst thou do such a deed for all the world?

EMILIA   Why, would not you?

DESDEMONA   No, by this heavenly light!

EMILIA   Nor I neither by this heavenly light;
I might do it as well in the dark.

DESDEMONA Wouldst thou do such a deed for all the world?   65

EMILIA   The world's a huge thing; it is a great price
For a small vice.

DESDEMONA In troth, I think thou wouldst not.

EMILIA   In troth, I think I should; and undo't when I had done. Marry, I
would not do such a thing for a joint-ring, nor for measures of lawn, nor   70
for gowns, petticoats, nor caps, nor any petty exhibition. But for all the

72 *Ud's* God's

73 *venture purgatory for it* risk going to purgatory rather than straight to heaven

79 *to the vantage* in addition.   *store* populate

82 *slack their duties* do not give their wives sexual fulfilment

83 *And pour … foreign laps* give the sexual pleasure they owe their wives to other women

84 *peevish* bad-tempered

86 *scant our former having in despite* reduce our allowance out of spite

87 *galls* feelings of bitterness.   *grace* the capacity to forgive

89 *sense* feelings

92 *sport* sexual pleasure

93 *affection* passion

94 *frailty* weakness

98 *instruct us so* show us by example

99 *uses* habit

100 *Not to … bad mend* not to copy bad ways but to learn how to be made better by them

What kind of relationship do Desdemona and Emilia have here? Do they speak as equals or are there still indications that Emilia serves Desdemona? Do the two have a bond in any way as a result their relationships with their partners?

Emilia (Zoe Wanamaker) prepares
Desdemona (Imogen Stubbs) for bed

Compare the differing attitudes towards men and marriage shown by Desdemona and Emilia. How do these attitudes compare with the ones these characters have shown in other parts of the play?

Othello sends Desdemona to bed telling her to dismiss Emilia. Desdemona is in a melancholy mood and sings a song about unhappy love. She and Emilia talk about fidelity in marriage.

whole world? Ud's pity, who would not make her husband a cuckold, to make him a monarch? I should venture purgatory for it.

DESDEMONA Beshrew me if I would do such a wrong for the whole world!

EMILIA   Why, the wrong is but a wrong i' the world; and having the world   75
for your labour, 'tis a wrong in your own world, and you might quickly
make it right.

DESDEMONA I do not think there is any such woman.

EMILIA   Yes, a dozen; and as many to the vantage as would store the world
they played for.   80
But I do think it is their husbands' faults
If wives do fall. Say that they slack their duties,
And pour our treasures into foreign laps;
Or else break out in peevish jealousies,
Throwing restraint upon us; or say they strike us,   85
Or scant our former having in despite –
Why, we have galls; and though we have some grace,
Yet have we some revenge. Let husbands know
Their wives have sense like them: they see, and smell,
And have their palates both for sweet and sour,   90
As husbands have. What is it that they do
When they change us for others? Is it sport?
I think it is. And doth affection breed it?
I think it doth. Is 't frailty that thus errs?
It is so too. And have not we affections,   95
Desires for sport, and frailty, as men have?
Then let them use us well; else let them know
The ills we do, their ills instruct us so.

DESDEMONA Good night, good night. Heaven me such uses send,
Not to pick bad from bad, but by bad mend.   100

[*Exeunt*

5:1

Cassio leaves Bianca's house and is attacked in the darkness by Roderigo. Cassio wounds Roderigo, but unseen Iago stabs Cassio and then runs off. Lodovico and Gratiano arrive and try to sort out what has happened. Iago finds the wounded Roderigo and appears to kill him.

1	*bulk* projecting part of a building
	straight straightaway
2	*rapier* sword
	bare unsheathed
	put it home thrust it deep into him
4	*It makes us or it mars us* our plan will succeed or it will ruin us
6	*miscarry* fail
8	*devotion* enthusiasm
11	*quat* boil
	to the sense until it is raw
14	*makes my gain* I win either way
	Live Roderigo if Roderigo lives
15	*calls me … restitution large* will call on me to repay all the money I owe him
16	*bobbed* swindled
19–20	*He hath a daily beauty … makes me ugly* Cassio has a nobility and fineness of character compared to which Iago appears rough and crude.
21	*unfold* expose
23	*gait* walk
24	*That thrust had been mine enemy indeed* that thrust would have killed me
25	*But that my coat is better than* i.e. Cassio is wearing a protective coat.
26	*I will make proof of thine* I will test yours

This part of the scene takes place in darkness and the words and actions indicate the fact that the characters cannot see each other. In the Shakespearean theatre, this would have been performed in daylight and the impression of darkness would have been created entirely through the language of the play. Which lines act as 'stage directions' in this way?

31	*brave* noble
33	*Minion* literally a lowly servant (used here ironically as a term of endearment)
34	*your unblest fate hies* your unholy fate rapidly approaches

5:1   *Enter* **IAGO** *and* **RODERIGO**

IAGO   Here, stand behind this bulk; straight will he come.
                    Wear thy good rapier bare, and put it home.
                    Quick, quick! Fear nothing – I'll be at thy elbow.
                    It makes us, or it mars us: think on that,
                    And fix most firm they resolution.   5

RODERIGO   Be near at hand; I may miscarry in 't.

IAGO   Here, at thy hand. Be bold, and take thy stand.   *[Moves aside*

RODERIGO   I have no great devotion to the deed,
                    And yet he hath given me satisfying reasons.
                    'Tis but a man gone. Forth my sword! He dies!   10

IAGO   I have rubbed this young quat almost to the sense,
                    And he grows angry. Now, whether he kill Cassio,
                    Or Cassio him, or each do kill the other,
                    Every way makes my gain. Live Roderigo,
                    He calls me a restitution large   15
                    Of gold and jewels that I bobbed from him
                    As gifts to Desdemona.
                    It must not be. If Cassio do remain
                    He hath a daily beauty in his life
                    That makes me ugly; and besides, the Moor   20
                    May unfold me to him – there stand I in much peril.
                    No, he must die. Be 't so – I hear him coming.

                              Enter **CASSIO**

RODERIGO   I know his gait – 'tis he. Villain, thou diest!

                                                                        [Thrusts at **CASSIO**

CASSIO   That thrust had been mine enemy indeed,
                    But that my coat is better than thou know'st.   25
                    I will make proof of thine.

                                          *[***CASSIO** *and* **RODERIGO** *fight*

RODERIGO   Oh, I am slain!

CASSIO   I am maimed for ever. Help, ho! Murder, murder! *[Exit* **IAGO**

                              Enter **OTHELLO**

OTHELLO   The voice of Cassio! Iago keeps his word.

RODERIGO   Oh, villain that I am!

OTHELLO   It is even so.

CASSIO   Oh help, ho! Light! A surgeon!   30

OTHELLO   'Tis he! Oh brave Iago, honest and just,
                    That hast such noble sense of thy friend's wrong,
                    Thou teachest me. Minion, your dear lies dead,
                    And your unblest fate hies. Strumpet, I come!

35 *Forth … blotted* the charms that your eyes have given are blotted from my heart

37 *watch* watchmen
   passage passers by

> As Iago leaves, having wounded Cassio, Othello enters. This section can be quite difficult to perform convincingly on the stage and often modern productions cut it completely. It has been suggested that in the Shakespearean theatre Othello would enter on the upper level looking down on the action as if from an upstairs window. Think about ways in which you could present this part of the scene, sketching out the stage layout, position and movement on stage of the characters and the lighting effects used.

38 *direful* anguished

42 *heavy* dark and gloomy

43 *counterfeits* people pretending to be hurt (i.e. in order to lure people into the darkness where they can be attacked)

44 *come into the cry* go to where the cry is coming from

47 *in his shirt* suggesting he has just got up

53 *What are you here* who's there

54 *spoiled* fatally wounded
   undone destroyed

Forth of my heart those charms, thine eyes, are blotted   **35**
Thy bed, lust-stained, shall with lust's blood be spotted.   *[Exit*

Enter LODOVICO *and* GRATIANO

CASSIO   What, ho? No watch? No passage? Murder, murder!

GRATIANO   'Tis some mischance: the voice is very direful.

CASSIO   Oh, help!

LODOVICO   Hark!   **40**

RODERIGO   Oh, wretched villain.

LODOVICO   Two or three groan. It is a heavy night.
These may be counterfeits. Let's think 't unsafe.
To come into the cry without more help.

RODERIGO   Nobody come? Then shall I bleed to death.   **45**

LODOVICO   Hark!

Enter IAGO *with a light*

GRATIANO   Here's one comes in his shirt, with light and weapons.

IAGO   Who's there? Whose noise is this that cries on murder?

LODOVICO   We do not know.

IAGO   Do not you hear a cry?

CASSIO   Here, here! For heaven's sake, help me!

IAGO   What's the matter?   **50**

GRATIANO   This is Othello's Ancient, as I take it.

LODOVICO   The same indeed, a very valiant fellow.

IAGO   What are you here, that cry so grievously?

CASSIO   Iago? Oh, I am spoiled, undone by villains!
Give me some help.   **55**

IAGO   Oh me, Lieutenant! What villains have done this?

CASSIO   I think that one of them is hereabout
And cannot make away.

IAGO   Oh treacherous villains!
[To LODOVICO *and* GRATIANO*]* What are you there? Come in, and give
some help.

RODERIGO   Oh, help me there!   **60**

CASSIO   That's one of them.

IAGO   Oh murderous slave! Oh villain!

[Stabs RODERIGO

RODERIGO   Oh damned Iago! Oh inhuman dog!   *[Faints*

IAGO   Kill men i' the dark? Where be these bloody thieves?
How silent is this town! Ho, murder, murder!

66 *As you … praise us* test us and we will prove to be friends

69 *I cry you mercy* I beg your pardon

> *Iago needs to convince others of his innocent concern for Cassio here. How do his actions and his words maintain the appearance of concern for his wounded 'friend'?*

78 *notable* notorious

79 *mangled* wounded

82 *Lend me a garter* i.e. to secure the bandage he has put on his leg

85 *trash* i.e. Bianca

86 *a party in* involved in

94 *accidents* sudden events

LODOVICO *and* GRATIANO *approach*

What may you be? Are you of good or evil? 65

LODOVICO As you shall prove us, praise us.

IAGO Signor Lodovico?

LODOVICO He, sir.

IAGO I cry you mercy. Here's Cassio hurt by villains.

GRATIANO Cassio? 70

IAGO How is it, brother?

CASSIO My leg is cut in two.

IAGO Marry, heaven forbid!
Light, gentlemen. I'll bind it with my shirt.

Enter BIANCA

BIANCA What is the matter, ho? Who is 't that cried?

IAGO Who is 't that cried? 75

BIANCA Oh, my dear Cassio! My sweet Cassio!
Oh, Cassio, Cassio, Cassio!

IAGO Oh notable strumpet! – Cassio, may you suspect
Who they should be that have thus mangled you?

CASSIO No. 80

GRATIANO I am sorry to find you thus. I have been to seek you.

IAGO Lend me a garter. So. Oh for a chair
To bear him easily hence.

BIANCA Alas, he faints!
Oh Cassio, Cassio, Cassio!

IAGO Gentlemen all, I do suspect this trash 85
To be a party in this injury. –
Patience awhile, good Cassio. – Come, come,
Lend me a light. Know we this face, or no?
Alas, my friend and my dear countryman
Roderigo? No – yes, sure – Oh heaven, Roderigo! 90

GRATIANO What, of Venice?

IAGO Even he, sir. Did you know him?

GRATIANO Know him? Ay.

IAGO Signor Gratiano? I cry your gentle pardon.
These bloody accidents must excuse my manners
That so neglected you.

GRATIANO I am glad to see you. 95

IAGO How do you, Cassio? – Oh, a chair, a chair!

GRATIANO Roderigo?

IAGO He, he, 'tis he.

98	*well said* well done
101	*Save you your labour* don't bother trying to help him
102	*malice* ill-feeling
104	*bear him out o' the air* take him indoors
106	*gastness of* frightened look in
107	*you* i.e. Bianca
	stare look terrified
	we shall hear more anon we will hear more from you soon
109–10	*guiltiness will … out of use* her guilt can be seen even though she says nothing
114	*quite dead* Iago is mistaken here.
116	*fruits of whoring* consequences of going with whores
119	*but I therefore shake not* I'm not shaking because of guilt
120	*charge* order

What techniques does Iago employ to make Bianca look guilty? Identify particular lines that slant the evidence and create a particular viewpoint of Bianca's role.

121	*Oh fie upon thee, strumpet* shame on you, whore
124	*dressed* bandaged
125	*another tale* a different story
128	*afore* ahead
129	*fordoes me quite* destroys me completely

Compare this scene with the opening scene of the play which also takes place under cover of darkness. Are there any similarities?

Iago's plan reaches its climax as Roderigo attempts to kill Cassio but instead is wounded by him. Iago wounds Cassio and then apparently kills Roderigo and manages to make it look as if Bianca is the cause of all the trouble.

Enter ATTENDANTS *with chair*

Oh, that's well said – the chair.
Some good man bear him carefully from hence.
I'll fetch the General's surgeon. [*To* BIANCA] For you, mistress,   **100**
Save you your labour. [*To* CASSIO] He that lies slain here, Cassio,
Was my dear friend. What malice was between you?

CASSIO   None in the world; nor do I know the man.

IAGO   What, look you pale? – Oh, bear him out o' the air.

CASSIO *and* RODERIGO *are carried off*

Stay you, good gentlemen. – Look you pale, mistress? –   **105**
Do you perceive the gastness of her eye?
Nay, if you stare, we shall hear more anon. –
Behold her well; I pray you look upon her;
Do you see, gentlemen? Nay, guiltiness will speak
Though tongues were out of use.   **110**

Enter EMILIA

EMILIA   Alas, what is the matter? What is the matter, husband?

IAGO   Cassio hath here been set on in the dark
By Roderigo and fellows that are scaped.
He's almost slain and Roderigo quite dead.

EMILIA   Alas, good gentleman! Alas, good Cassio!   **115**

IAGO   This is the fruits of whoring. Prithee, Emilia,
Go know of Cassio where he supped tonight.
[*To* BIANCA] What, do you shake at that?

BIANCA   He supped at my house; but I therefore shake not.

IAGO   Oh, did he so? I charge you go with me.   **120**

EMILIA   Oh fie upon thee, strumpet!

BIANCA   I am no strumpet, but of life as honest
As you that thus abuse me.

EMILIA   As I? Fie upon thee!

IAGO   Kind gentlemen, let's go see poor Cassio dressed.
[*To* BIANCA] Come, mistress, you must tell 's another tale.   **125**
Emilia, run you to the citadel
And tell my lord and lady what hath happened.   [*Exit* EMILIA
Will you go on afore?

                         [*Exeunt all but* IAGO

                This is the night
That either makes me, or fordoes me quite.   [*Exit*

5:2

Othello approaches the bed where Desdemona is asleep and he looks at her, admiring her beauty. She wakes and pleads with him to let her live. He refuses to listen and smothers her. Emilia discovers the dying Desdemona and calls for help realising that Othello has murdered her. Montano, Gratiano and Iago arrive and Iago's scheming is uncovered. He stabs Emilia and runs away but is caught and brought back. Othello, realising what he has done, kills himself.

1   *the cause* the reason for killing her (i.e. her adultery)

5   *monumental alabaster* a white stone used for carving effigies on tombs

7   *Put out the light, and then put out the light* put out the torch I am carrying and then put out Desdemona's light (i.e. kill her)

8   *flaming minister* the torch

10   *repent me* regret my action

11   *cunning'st pattern of excelling nature* cleverly created picture of nature at its most perfect

12   *Promethean heat* life-giving fire (In Greek mythology, Prometheus stole fire from the gods and gave it to men.)

13   *relume* re-light

14   *vital growth* life

16   *balmy* fragrant

17   *Justice to break her sword* me to not carry out justice by killing you (Othello sees himself as the figure of Justice about to carry out a legitimate sentence.)

20   *So sweet was ne'er so fatal* a kiss was never so sweet and so deadly

21   *heavenly* divine

What is Othello's mood here? How does this compare with the last time we saw him in Act 5 Scene 1 (lines 31–6)? Is his mood different? What do you notice about the vocabulary and imagery he uses? How should the actor playing Othello be seen here? Out of control? Coldly cruel? Hurt and suffering?

27   *Unreconciled … grace* that you have not yet confessed and been forgiven for

28   *Solicit* pray
      straight immediately

30   *walk by* walk nearby

32   *forfend* forbid

39   *fatal* very dangerous

5:2   DESDEMONA *in her bed asleep; enter* OTHELLO *with a light*

OTHELLO   It is the cause, it is the cause, my soul.
           Let me not name it to you, you chaste stars!
           It is the cause. Yet I'll not shed her blood,
           Nor scar that whiter skin of hers than snow,
           And smooth as monumental alabaster;   5
           Yet she must die, else she'll betray more men.
           Put out the light, and then put out the light.
           If I quench thee, thou flaming minister,
           I can again thy former light restore,
           Should I repent me; but once put out thy light,   10
           Thou cunning'st pattern of excelling nature,
           I know not where is that Promethean heat
           That can thy light relume. When I have plucked thy rose
           I cannot give it vital growth again;
           It needs must wither. I'll smell thee on the tree.   [*Kisses her*   15
           Oh balmy breath, that dost almost persuade
           Justice to break her sword! One more, one more!
           Be thus when thou art dead, and I will kill thee
           And love thee after. One more, and that's the last!
           So sweet was ne'er so fatal. I must weep,   20
           But they are cruel tears. This sorrow's heavenly –
           It strikes where it doth love. She wakes.

DESDEMONA Who's there? Othello?

OTHELLO   Ay, Desdemona.

DESDEMONA Will you come to bed, my lord?

OTHELLO   Have you prayed tonight, Desdemon?

DESDEMONA   Ay, my lord.   25

OTHELLO   If you bethink yourself of any crime
           Unreconciled as yet to heaven and grace,
           Solicit for it straight.

DESDEMONA Alack, my lord, what may you mean by that?

OTHELLO   Well, do it, and be brief; I will walk by.   30
           I would not kill thy unpreparèd spirit;
           No, heavens forfend! I would not kill thy soul.

DESDEMONA Talk you of killing?

OTHELLO   Ay, I do.

DESDEMONA Then heaven have mercy on me!   35

OTHELLO   Amen, with all my heart!

DESDEMONA If you say so, I hope you will not kill me.

OTHELLO   Hum!

DESDEMONA And yet I fear you; for you're fatal then

42   *They are loves I bear to you* the only sins I have committed are those done because of my love for you

45   *nether* lower

46   *frame* body

47   *portents* ominous signs

48   *do not point on me* are not a sign of what will happen to me

53   *perjury* lying on oath

54   *presently* immediately

56   *article* each sin

57–8 *Cannot remove … withal* would not remove my belief that you are guilty

61   *Offend* sin against

62   *general warranty* permission

65   *stone* turn to stone

72   *Unlawfully* had illicit sex

The dramatic tension builds up as Desdemona questions the reasons for Othello's passion. If you were acting the role of Othello here how would you present the character? Would you give an impression of calm control, of an executioner administering justice? Would you show a character whose emotions are in turmoil and who is desperately trying to stick to his chosen path? How would your interpretation be conveyed through tone of voice, actions, looks? Would you take into account Desdemona's description of his eyes rolling (line 40), lip biting (line 45) and shaking (line 46)? Many modern productions ignore these details when presenting Othello at this point. Why do you thinks this is?

When your eyes roll so. Why I should fear I know not,   **40**
Since guiltiness I know not; but yet I feel I fear.

OTHELLO   Think on thy sins.

DESDEMONA   They are loves I bear to you.

OTHELLO   Ay, and for that thou diest.

DESDEMONA That death's unnatural that kills for loving.
Alas, why gnaw you so your nether lip?   **45**
Some bloody passion shakes your very frame.
These are portents; but yet I hope, I hope.
They do not point on me.

OTHELLO   Peace, and be still!

DESDEMONA I will so. What's the matter?

OTHELLO   That handkerchief which I so loved, and gave thee,   **50**
Thou gav'st to Cassio.

DESDEMONA   No, by my life and soul!
Send for the man and ask him.

OTHELLO   Sweet soul, take heed,
Take heed of perjury: thou art on thy death-bed.

DESDEMONA Ay, but not yet to die.

OTHELLO   Presently.
Therefore confess thee freely of thy sin;   **55**
For to deny each article with oath
Cannot remove nor choke the strong conception
That I do groan withal. Thou art to die.

DESDEMONA Then Lord have mercy on me.

OTHELLO   I say, Amen.

DESDEMONA And have you mercy too! I never did   **60**
Offend you in my life – never loved Cassio
But with such general warranty of heaven
As I might love. I never gave him token.

OTHELLO   By heaven, I saw my handkerchief in his hand!
Oh perjured woman, thou dost stone my heart,   **65**
And mak'st me call what I intend to do
A murder, which I thought a sacrifice.
I saw the handkerchief.

DESDEMONA   He found it then.
I never gave it him. Send for him hither.
Let him confess a truth.

OTHELLO   He hath confessed.   **70**

DESDEMONA What, my lord?

OTHELLO   That he hath used thee –

DESDEMONA   How? Unlawfully?

74 *ta'en order for 't* carried it out

75 *my fear interprets* I am afraid and I begin to understand

76 *Had all his hairs been lives* if he had as many lives as he has hairs on his head

77 *stomach* appetite

78 *undone* finished

83 *strive* struggle

84 *Being done, there is no pause* now that I have started I cannot stop

> *The action reaches its terrible and dramatic climax as Othello smothers Desdemona. In many productions, Desdemona is passive as Othello kills her. In the 1995 film version, though, Desdemona struggles and kicks out at Othello (Laurence Fishburne), while in the 1989 RSC production Imogen Stubbs fights, struggles and attempts to escape from the room and Othello (Willard White) has to physically overpower her. What different effects are achieved through such different interpretations? How would you present the murder of Desdemona if you were producing the play? What dramatic effect is achieved by Emilia's* **My lord, my lord!** *just at the moment Othello smothers her?*

Othello kills Desdemona

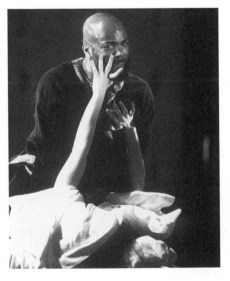

95 *like* likely

96 *The noise was high* there was a lot of noise during the attack on Cassio

101 *insupportable* unbearable

103–4 *that … alteration* the world would split open at the change (i.e. Desdemona's death)

OTHELLO   Ay.

DESDEMONA He will not say so!

OTHELLO   No, his mouth is stopped.
Honest Iago hath ta'en order for't.

DESDEMONA Oh, my fear interprets. What, is he dead?   75

OTHELLO   Had all his hairs been lives, my great revenge
Had stomach for them all.

DESDEMONA Alas, he is betrayed, and I undone!

OTHELLO   Out, strumpet! Weep'st thou for him to my face?

DESDEMONA Oh banish me, my lord, but kill me not.   80

OTHELLO   Down, strumpet!

DESDEMONA Kill me tomorrow: let me live tonight!

OTHELLO   Nay, if you strive –

DESDEMONA But half an hour!

OTHELLO   Being done, there is no pause.

DESDEMONA But while I say one prayer!

OTHELLO   It is too late.   85

DESDEMONA Oh Lord, Lord, Lord!

He smothers her

EMILIA [*Off-stage*] My lord, my lord! What, ho! My lord, my lord!

OTHELLO   What noise is this? Not dead? Not yet quite dead?
I that am cruel am yet merciful:
I would not have thee linger in they pain.   90
So, so.

EMILIA [*Off-stage*] What, ho! My lord, my lord!

OTHELLO   Who's there?

EMILIA [*Off-stage*] Oh, good my lord, I would speak a word with you.

OTHELLO Yes – 'tis Emilia – by and by. – She's dead.
'Tis like she comes to speak of Cassio's death: 95
The noise was high. Ha! No more moving?
Still as the grave. Shall she come in? Were 't good?
I think she stirs again. No. What's best to do?
If she come in, she'll speak to my wife.
My wife! My wife! What wife? I have no wife.   100
Oh, insupportable! Oh heavy hour!
Methinks it should be now a huge eclipse
Of sun and moon, and that the affrighted globe
Should yawn at alteration.

EMILIA [*Off-stage*]   I do beseech you
That I may speak with you, oh good my lord.   105

111 *error* wandering off course (Compare with Act 2 Scene 3, line 160 – the idea that the moon made people mad.)

112 *wont* accustomed

117–18 *Then murder's … grows harsh* the murder plan has gone wrong and my revenge no longer sweet

121 *Out and alas* an exclamation of grief

127 *Commend me to* give my love to

As Emilia approaches, Othello says **Let me the curtains draw.** *Why are the curtains around Desdemona's bed an important aspect of the staging? Desdemona's 'revival' needs careful handling on the stage otherwise it runs the risk of appearing comic. Think about ways in which Desdemona's last few words can be delivered most effectively.*

128 *how should she be murdered* how can she have been murdered

134 *folly* adultery

135 *belie* slander

OTHELLO   I had forgot thee. Oh, come in, Emilia.
　　　Soft, by and by. – Let me the curtains draw. –
　　　Where art thou? [*Unlocks the door*] What's the matter with thee now?

Enter EMILIA

EMILIA   Oh my good lord, yonder's foul murders done!

OTHELLO   What? Now?

EMILIA　　　　　　But now, my lord.　　　　　　　　　110

OTHELLO   It is the very error of the moon;
　　　She comes more nearer earth than she was wont,
　　　And makes men mad.

EMILIA   Cassio, my lord, hath killed a young Venetian
　　　Called Roderigo.

OTHELLO　　　　　　Roderigo killed?　　　　　　　115
　　　And Cassio killed?

EMILIA　　　　　　　No, Cassio is not killed.

OTHELLO   Not Cassio killed? Then murder's out of tune,
　　　And sweet revenge grows harsh.

DESDEMONA Oh, falsely, falsely murdered.

EMILIA　　　　　　　　　Oh Lord! What cry is that?

OTHELLO   That? What?　　　　　　　　　　　　120

EMILIA   Out and alas, that was my lady's voice!　　*[Draws back the curtain*
　　　Help, help, ho! Help! – Oh, lady, speak again!
　　　Sweet Desdemona, oh sweet mistress, speak!

DESDEMONA A guiltless death I die.

EMILIA   Oh, who hath done this deed?　　　　　125

DESDEMONA Nobody – I myself. Farewell.
　　　Commend me to my kind lord. Oh farewell!　　　*[Dies*

OTHELLO   Why, how should she be murdered?

EMILIA　　　　　　　　Alas, who knows?

OTHELLO   You heard her say herself it was not I.

EMILIA   She said so. I must needs report the truth.　　130

OTHELLO   She's like a liar gone to burning hell.
　　　'Twas I that killed her.

EMILIA　　　　　Oh, the more angel she,
　　　And you the blacker devil!

OTHELLO   She turned to folly, and she was a whore.

EMILIA   Thou dost belie her, and thou art a devil.　　135

OTHELLO   She was false as water.

EMILIA　　　　　　Thou art rash as fire to say
　　　That she was false. Oh, she was heavenly true!

138	*top* have sex with
	else if you think this isn't true
141	*extremity* extreme punishment
145	*chrysolite* topaz
150	*iterance* repetition
151	*made mocks with love* played games with
155	*pernicious* wicked and destructive
156	*to the heart* absolutely
159	*fond of* foolishly infatuated by
	most filthy bargain disgusting marriage
161	*Peace, you were best* You'd better shut up
163	*gull* gullible fool
	dolt idiot
165	*I care not for thy sword* I don't care if you threaten me with your sword
	I'll make thee known I'll tell everybody what you have done
170	*lay their murders on your neck* blame you for the murders they committed

What is Emilia's reaction when she realises what has happened? What tone does she use in speaking to Othello? Does she sound angry? Distraught? Shocked? Bewildered? Disbelieving? The word 'husband' is repeated again and again as Emilia echoes Othello's words. What dramatic effect is created through this repetition? A sense of disbelief? Anger? Realisation of what has happened?

OTHELLO	Cassio did top her: ask thy husband else.
	Oh, I were damned beneath all depth in hell
	But that I did proceed upon just grounds **140**
	To this extremity. Thy husband knew it all.
EMILIA	My husband?
OTHELLO	Thy husband.
EMILIA	That she was false to wedlock?
OTHELLO	Ay, with Cassio. Had she been true,
	If heaven would make me such another world
	Of one entire and perfect chrysolite, **145**
	I'd not have sold her for it.
EMILIA	My husband?
OTHELLO	Ay, 'twas he that told me on her first.
	An honest man he is, and hates the slime
	That sticks on filthy deeds.
EMILIA	My husband?
OTHELLO	What needs this iterance, woman? I say thy husband. **150**
EMILIA	Oh, mistress, villainy hath made mocks with love!
	My husband say she was false?
OTHELLO	He, woman;
	I say thy husband; dost understand the word?
	My friend, thy husband, honest, honest Iago.
EMILIA	If he say so, may his pernicious soul **155**
	Rot half a grain a day! He lies to the heart.
	She was too fond of her most filthy bargain.
OTHELLO	Ha?
EMILIA	Do thy worst.
	This deed of thine is no more worthy heaven **160**
	Than thou wast worthy her.
OTHELLO	Peace, you were best.
EMILIA	Thou hast not half that power to do me harm
	As I have to be hurt. Oh gull! Oh dolt!
	As ignorant as dirt! Thou hast done a deed –

                       OTHELLO *starts to draw his sword*

	I care not for thy sword; I'll make thee known **165**
	Though I lost twenty lives. Help! Help, ho! Help!
	The Moor hath killed my mistress! Murder! Murder!

       Enter **MONTANO, GRATIANO, IAGO** *and* **ATTENDANTS**

MONTANO	What is the matter? How now, General?
EMILIA	Oh, are you come, Iago? You have done well,
	That men must lay their murders on your neck. **170**
GRATIANO	What is the matter?

177 *apt* likely

183 *charm my tongue* put a spell on (i.e. to make it quiet)

186 *forfend* forbid

187 *set the murder on* caused the murder

194 *charge* order

196 *proper* fitting

197 *perchance* perhaps

201 *scarce did know* hardly recognised
uncle Gratiano (i.e. Desdemona's uncle)

203 *shows* appears

205 *Thy match was mortal to him* your marriage caused his death

206 *Shore* cut
thread life
Did he live if he were alive

207 *do a desperate turn* do something desperate (i.e. kill himself)

208 *better angel* guardian angel

209 *reprobance* damnation

EMILIA	Disprove this villain, if thou be'st a man.	
	He says thou toldst him that his wife was false.	
	I know thou didst not: thou art not such a villain.	
	Speak, for my heart is full.	**175**
IAGO	I told him what I thought, and told no more	
	Than what he found himself was apt and true.	
EMILIA	But did you ever tell him she was false?	
IAGO	I did.	
EMILIA	You told a lie, an odious damnèd lie!	**180**
	Upon my soul, a lie! A wicked lie!	
	She, false with Cassio? Did you say with Cassio?	
IAGO	With Cassio, mistress. Go to, charm your tongue.	
EMILIA	I will not charm my tongue; I am bound to speak:	
	My mistress here lies murdered in her bed.	**185**
ALL	O heavens forfend!	
EMILIA	And your reports have set the murder on.	
OTHELLO	Nay, stare not, masters. It is true indeed.	
GRATIANO	'Tis a strange truth.	
MONTANO	Oh monstrous act!	
EMILIA	Villainy, villainy, villainy!	**190**
	I think upon 't – I think I smell 't – oh villainy!	
	I thought so then. I'll kill myself for grief.	
	Oh villainy, villainy!	
IAGO	What, are you mad? I charge you get you home.	
EMILIA	Good gentlemen, let me have leave to speak.	**195**
	'Tis proper I obey him, but not now.	
	Perchance, Iago, I will ne'er go home.	
OTHELLO	Oh, oh, oh! *[Falls on the bed*	
EMILIA	Nay, lay thee down and roar,	
	For thou hast killed the sweetest innocent	
	That e'er did lift up eye.	
OTHELLO [*Rising*]	Oh she was foul!	**200**
	I scarce did know you, uncle. There lies your niece,	
	Whose breath indeed these hands have newly stopped.	
	I know this act shows horrible and grim.	
GRATIANO	Poor Desdemon! I am glad thy father's dead:	
	Thy match was mortal to him, and pure grief	**205**
	Shore his old thread in twain. Did he live now,	
	This sight would make him do a desperate turn;	
	Yea, curse his better angel from his side,	
	And fall to reprobance.	
OTHELLO	'Tis pitiful; but yet Iago knows	**210**

211	*the act of shame* adultery
213	*gratify his amorous works* reward his love-making
214	*recognizance* token
216	*antique* old
219	*Zounds* by God's wounds (an oath) *'Twill out* the truth will come out *I peace* i.e. no way will I be quiet
220	*as liberal as the north* as freely as the north wind blows
224	*Fie* shame on you
225	*dull* stupid
226	*by fortune* by chance
228	*belonged* was appropriate
233	*coxcomb* fool
234–5	*Are there … thunder* are there no thunderbolts in heaven to punish the wicked
239	*notorious* obvious

Look at lines 180–235. Iago becomes increasingly desperate to keep Emilia quiet in this section. Pick out each of his lines which indicate his attempts to silence her culminating in **Villainous whore!** *(line 229)* and **Filth, thou liest!** *(line 231)*. Notice how he tries to keep her quiet and as she defies him his tone becomes more and more threatening. Think about how each of Iago's lines directed at Emilia could be spoken to build up the sense of menace in his voice as he begins to loose control of the situation.

	That she with Cassio hath the act of shame	
	A thousand times committed. Cassio confessed it,	
	And she did gratify his amorous works	
	With that recognizance and pledge of love	
	Which I first gave her. I saw it in his hand.	215
	It was a handkerchief, an antique token	
	My father gave my mother.	

EMILIA   Oh God! Oh heavenly God!

IAGO   Zounds, hold your peace!

EMILIA   'Twill out, 'twill out. I peace?
No, I will speak as liberal as the north.   220
Let heaven, and men, and devils, let them all,
All, all, cry shame against me – yet I'll speak.

IAGO   Be wise, and get you home.

EMILIA   I will not.

> IAGO *draws his sword*

GRATIANO   Fie! Your sword upon a woman?

EMILIA   Oh thou dull Moor, that handkerchief thou speak'st of   225
I found by fortune, and did give my husband;
For often with a solemn earnestness –
More than indeed belonged to such a trifle –
He begged of me to steal it.

IAGO   Villainous whore!

EMILIA   She give it Cassio? No, alas, I found it,   230
And I did give 't my husband.

IAGO   Filth, thou liest!

EMILIA   By heaven I do not, I do not, gentlemen.
Oh murderous coxcomb! What should such a fool
Do with so good a wife?

OTHELLO   Are there no stones in heaven
But what serves for the thunder? Precious villain!   235

> OTHELLO *runs at* IAGO. MONTANO *disarms* OTHELLO.
> IAGO *stabs* EMILIA *and runs out.*

GRATIANO   The woman falls – sure he hath killed his wife.

EMILIA   Ay, ay. Oh lay me by my mistress' side.

GRATIANO   He's gone, but his wife's killed.

MONTANO   'Tis a notorious villain. Take you this weapon,
Which I have recovered from the Moor.   240
Come, guard the door without. Let him not pass,
But kill him rather. I'll after the same villain,
For 'tis a damnèd slave.

> [*Exeunt all but* OTHELLO *and* EMILIA

244 *puny whipster* puny wretch
gets my sword can take my sword from me

245 *why should honour outlive honesty* why should a man's honour survive when he has no virtue left

246 *bode* foretell

247 *play the swan* Swans were supposed to sing only once, just before they died.

250 *So come my soul to bliss* so may my soul come to heaven

253 *sword of Spain* Spanish swords were renowned for their quality. *ice-brook's temper* Steel was tempered (made hard) by being plunged red-hot into ice-cold water.

256 *perforce* inevitably

258 *naked* unarmed

264 *stop* power to stop me

267 *butt* goal

268 *sea-mark* marker buoy
utmost sail last voyage

269 *lost* pointless

270 *Man but a rush* aim only a reed

271 *retires* retreats

272 *ill-starred* ill-fated

273 *at compt* at the final reckoning (i.e. Judgement Day)

277 *cursèd slave* Othello is referring to himself.

280 *steep-down* sheer

Look at Othello's speech (lines 259–81). What is the dramatic importance of this speech? How would you describe his mood at this point in the play? Does it change as his speech progresses?

OTHELLO   I am not valiant neither,
But every puny whipster gets my sword.
But why should honour outlive honesty?   245
Let it go all.

EMILIA   What did thy song bode, lady?
Hark, canst thou hear me? I will play the swan,
And die in music. [*Sings*] Willow, willow, willow.
[*Speaks*] Moor, she was chaste. She loved thee, cruel Moor,
So come my soul to bliss as I speak true.   250
So speaking as I think, alas, I die.   [*Dies*

OTHELLO   I have another weapon in this chamber;
It was a sword of Spain, the ice-brook's temper.
Oh, here it is. – Uncle, I must come forth.

GRATIANO [*Off-stage*] If thou attempt it, it will cost thee dear.   255
Thou hast no weapon, and perforce must suffer.

OTHELLO   Look in upon me then, and speak with me.
Or, naked as I am, I will assault thee.

Enter **GRATIANO**

GRATIANO   What is the matter?

OTHELLO   Behold, I have a weapon:
A better never did itself sustain   260
Upon a soldier's thigh. I have seen the day
That with this little arm, and this good sword,
I have made my way through more impediments
Than twenty times your stop. But, oh vain boast!
Who can control his fate? 'Tis not so now.   265
Be not afraid, though you do see me weaponed.
Here is my journey's end, here is my butt
And very sea-mark of my utmost sail.
Do you go back dismayed? 'Tis a lost fear:
Man but a rush against Othello's breast,   270
And he retires. Where should Othello go?   [*Goes to the bed*
Now, how dost thou look now? Oh ill-starred wench,
Pale as thy smock! When we shall meet at compt,
This look of thine will hurl my soul from heaven
And fiends will snatch at it. Cold, cold, my girl?   275
Even like thy chastity.
Oh cursèd, cursèd slave! Whip me, ye devils,
From the possession of this heavenly sight!
Blow me about in winds! Roast me in sulphur!
Wash me in steep-down gulfs of liquid fire!   280
Oh Desdemon! Dead Desdemon! Dead. Oh, oh!

284   *viper* i.e. Iago

285   *I look down towards his feet* The devil is said to have cloven
        hooves instead of feet.
        but that's a fable but that's only a story

289   *in my sense* the way I feel

> When Iago is caught and brought back, Othello attacks him saying **If that thou be'st a devil, I cannot kill thee** *(line 286). What tone of voice would Iago speak his reply* **I bleed, sir, but not killed** *(line 287)? Would he be gloating? Triumphant? Shaken? Sorry? Angry? What effect does his response have on Othello?*

291   *practice* plots

296   *consent in* plan together

> *Iago's final words* **Demand me nothing. What you know, you know** *are open to a wide range of interpretations. Does he spit these words with venom through gritted teeth? Is he completely impassive about all that has happened and his own situation? Does he smirk and show a gleam of triumph? Is he in pain and distressed? How would you play these lines if you were acting the role of Iago?*

304   *Torments* torture
        ope open

305   *thou dost best* you would be wise to say nothing

306   *befall'n* happened

309   *imports* is about

312   *heathenish and most gross* barbaric and outrageous

313   *discontented paper* letter revealing discontent

Enter **Lodovico**, **Montano**, **Cassio** *in a chair,*
and **Iago** *guarded by* **Officers**

Lodovico	Where is this rash and most unfortunate man?
Othello	That's he that was Othello: here I am.
Lodovico	Where is that viper? Bring the villain forth.
Othello	I look down towards his feet – but that's a fable.	285

If that thou be'st a devil, I cannot kill thee. [*Wounds* **Iago**

Lodovico Wrench his sword from him.

Officers *disarm* **Othello**

Iago   I bleed, sir, but not killed.

Othello I am not sorry neither. I'd have thee live,
For in my sense 'tis happiness to die.

Lodovico Oh thou, Othello, that was once so good,   290
Fall'n in the practice of a cursèd slave,
What shall be said to thee?

Othello   Why, anything:
An honourable murderer, if you will;
For naught I did in hate, but all in honour.

Lodovico This wretch hath part confessed his villainy.   295
Did you and he consent in Cassio's death?

Othello Ay.

Cassio Dear General, I never gave you cause.

Othello I do believe it, and I ask your pardon.
Will you, I pray, demand that demi-devil   300
Why he hath thus ensnared my soul and body?

Iago   Demand me nothing. What you know, you know.
From this time forth I never will speak word.

Lodovico What? Not to pray?

Gratiano   Torments will ope your lips.

Othello Well, thou dost best.   305

Lodovico Sir, you shall understand what hath befall'n,
Which, as I think, you know not. Here is a letter
Found in the pocket of the slain Roderigo,
And here another. The one of them imports
The death of Cassio, to be undertook   310
By Roderigo.

Othello Oh villain!

Cassio   Most heathenish and most gross!

Lodovico Now here's another discontented paper
Found in his pocket too: and this, it seems,
Roderigo meant to have sent this damnèd villain,   315

316	*belike* probably
	interim in the meantime
317	*satisfied him* calmed him down
	pernicious caitiff poisonous wretch
322	*wrought to his desire* was part of his plan
324	*upbraids* complains to
325	*Brave* provoke
	me upon the watch me while I was on guard
325–6	*whereon it came / That I was cast* as a result of which I was dismissed
331	*this slave* i.e. Iago
333	*hold him long* drag out his death
334	*You* i.e. Othello
	rest remain
337	*Soft you* wait a moment
340	*unlucky* ill-fated
341	*extenuate* excuse
345	*Perplexed* confused
346–7	*Like the base Indian … his tribe* i.e. not recognising the worth of what you have and throwing it away
347	*subdued* emotional
348	*Albeit unusèd to the melting mood* although not used to breaking down in tears
350	*med'cinable* healing
353	*traduced* dishonoured
354	*circumcisèd* unchristian
356	*period* end

‖ *Look at Othello's final speech. What is his mood and tone here?*
‖ *What dramatic effect does his suicide produce?*

Othello prepares to kill himself

190

But that, belike, Iago in the interim
Came in and satisfied him.

OTHELLO   Oh thou pernicious caitiff!
How came you, Cassio, by that handkerchief
That was my wife's?

CASSIO   I found it in my chamber;
And he himself confessed it but even now   320
That there he dropped it for a special purpose
Which wrought to his desire.

OTHELLO   Oh fool, fool, fool!

CASSIO   There is besides in Roderigo's letter,
How he upbraids Iago, that he made him
Brave me upon the watch; whereon it came   325
That I was cast; and even but now he spake,
After long seeming dead: Iago hurt him;
Iago set him on.

LODOVICO   You must forsake this room and go with us.
Your power and your command is taken off,   330
And Cassio rules in Cyprus. For this slave,
If there be any cunning cruelty
That can torment him much, and hold him long,
It shall be his. You shall close prisoner rest
Till that the nature of your fault be known   335
To the Venetian state. Come, bring away.

OTHELLO   Soft you, a word or two before you go.
I have done the state some service, and they know 't;
No more of that. I pray you, in your letters,
When you shall these unlucky deeds relate,   340
Speak of me as I am; nothing extenuate,
Nor set down aught in malice. Then must you speak
Of one that loved, not wisely, but too well;
Of one not easily jealous, but being wrought,
Perplexed in the extreme; of one whose hand,   345
Like the base Indian, threw a pearl away
Richer than all his tribe; of one whose subdued eyes,
Albeit unusèd to the melting mood,
Drop tears as fast as the Arabian trees
Their med'cinable gum. Set you down this.   350
And say besides, that in Aleppo once,
Where a malignant and a turbaned Turk
Beat a Venetian, and traduced the state,
I took by th' throat the circumcisèd dog
And smote him thus.   [*Stabs himself* 355

LODOVICO   Oh bloody period!

GRATIANO   All that is spoke is marred.

357 *thee* i.e. Desdemona

360 *Spartan dog* Spartan dogs were noted for their savagery in relentlessly pursuing their prey.

361 *fell* cruel

364 *keep* guard

365 *seize upon* confiscate

366 *succeed on you* passed on to

367 *censure* judgement

369 *straight* immediately
state Venetian senate

370 *heavy* sorrowful

Compare the final speech of Othello (lines 337–55) with his speech in Act 4 Scene 2 (lines 46–63) and Act 1 Scene 3 (lines 127–69). Do they have any features in common? Are there any differences?

Othello murders Desdemona but Emilia's arrival signals the unravelling of Iago's plot. He is unable to silence her before she reveals the full extent of his evil scheme. Othello, for the first time, sees Iago in his true light. Iago is caught and now, finally, Othello becomes aware of the deception that he has been a victim of and kills himself.

OTHELLO   I kissed thee ere I killed thee. No way but this,
          Killing myself, to die upon a kiss.   [*Falls on the bed and dies*

CASSIO   This did I fear, but thought he had no weapon;
          For he was great of heart.

LODOVICO [*To* IAGO]   O Spartan dog,   360
          More fell than anguish, hunger, or the sea!
          Look on the tragic loading of this bed:
          This is thy work. The object poisons sight;
          Let it be hid.

                    OFFICER *draws bed-curtains*

                    Gratiano, keep the house
          And seize upon the fortunes of the Moor,   365
          For they succeed on you. [*To* CASSIO] To you, Lord Governor,
          Remains the censure of this hellish villain:
          The time, the place, the torture. Oh, enforce it!
          Myself will straight aboard, and to the state
          This heavy act with heavy heart relate.   370

                                        [*Exeunt*

Othello

List of other titles in this series:

2003 titles:

Henry IV Part One
Lawrence Green
0-7487-6960-9

Henry IV Part One Teacher Resource Book
Lawrence Green
0-7487-6968-4

Julius Caesar
Mark Morris
0-7487-6959-5

Julius Caesar Teacher Resource Book
Mark Morris
0-7487-6967-6

Macbeth
Dinah Jurksaitis
0-7487-6955-2

Macbeth Teacher Resource Book
Dinah Jurksaitis
0-7487-6961-7

The Merchant of Venice
Tony Farrell
0-7487-6957-9

The Merchant of Venice Teacher Resource book
Tony Farrell
0-7487-6963-3

Romeo and Juliet
Duncan Beal
0-7487-6956-0

Romeo and Juliet Teacher Resource Book
Duncan Beal
0-7487-6962-5

The Tempest
David Stone
0-7487-6958-7

The Tempest Teacher Resource Book
David Stone
0-7487-6965-X

2004 titles:

Antony and Cleopatra
Tony Farrell
0-7487-8602-3

Antony and Cleopatra Teacher Resource Book
Tony Farrell
0-7487-8606-6

A Midsummer Night's Dream
Dinah Jurksaitis
0-7487-8604-X

A Midsummer Night's Dream Teacher Resource Book
Dinah Jurksaitis
0-7487-8608-2

Much Ado About Nothing
Lawrence Green
0-7487-8607-4

Much Ado About Nothing Teacher Resource Book
Lawrence Green
0-7487-8603-1

Othello
Steven Croft
0-7487-8601-5

Othello Teacher Resource Book
Steven Croft
0-7487-8605-8